MW01221878

Copyright Information Page

caused or alleged to be caused directly or indirectly by this report, nor do we make any claims or promises of your ability to generate income by using any of this information.

Tina A. Hull, Beyond Expectations Marketing, EMMF Publishing 869-669-7075
PO Box 115, Charlestown, St.Kitts and Nevis, Nevis, 00000
www.beyondexpectationsmarketing.com
Email: marketingandmassage@gmail.com
Twitter: @Marketmassage
Google +: Massage and Marketing (for tips and tricks)
Facebook:
https://www.facebook.com/massageandmarketing
LinkedIn:
http://www.linkedin.com/in/tinaahull/

DETERMINE YOUR BUSINESS VISION......... 67

    Revenue Plan 71

GOALS 75

MARKETING, MARKETING, MARKETING... 79

MARKETING OBJECTIVE 84

MARKETING PROCESS 87

EFFECTIVE SALES MESSAGE......................... 93

MARKETING COPY 103

FEATURE VERSUS BENEFIT......................... 109

DIFFERENTIATE YOURSELF FROM YOUR
COMPETITION! 111

YOUR REPUTATION 115

BRANDING YOU AND YOUR BUSINESS.... 119

BUSINESS CARDS 123

WEBSITES 125

SOCIAL MEDIA MARKETING 129

    LINKEDIN 131

    PINTEREST 136

Table of Contents

Copyright Information Page 1

Limits of Liability/Disclaimer of Warranty 3

Dedication 8

MY STORY 9

SETTING UP YOUR CLINIC 17

BASIC PERSONAL RULES 21

LAST MINUTE CANCELLATIONS AND NO-
SHOWS... 25

DOES MASSAGE THERAPY REALLY WORK?
.... 27

MINDSET.. 32

THE LAW OF ATTRACTION 36

MINDSET ABOUT MONEY AND SUCCESS .. 42

THE LAW OF COMPENSATION 48

TARGET MARKET... 52

WHO IS YOUR IDEAL CLIENT? 55

LIFETIME VALUE OF A CLIENT (LVC)......... 63

HOW TO CALCULATE LVC.............................. 65

I also used a linen service which picked up the dirty sheets and dropped off the clean sheets. You have to have enough sheets for 2 weeks worth of clients to do this though. Now you might be thinking, well I can throw a load or two of sheets in the laundry and perhaps you can. But ask yourself, is this a money making activity? If you are busy then having this service may be worth it. At the time I had to go to a Laundromat to do my clothes, so it was worth the aggravation, travel time and wait time. *Remember time is money.*

Turning Your Dream Business into a Reality!

A Marketing Guide for
Massage Therapists and Other Health
Professionals.

Tina A. Hull

Limits of Liability/Disclaimer of Warranty

FACEBOOK 141

TWITTER 144

QR CODES/MOBILE SITE/TEXT MESSAGING 146

PARETO'S LAW OR 80/20 RULE 152

WORD OF MOUTH MARKETING.................. 156

NETWORKING 163

STRATEGIC PLANNING 167

SOME PLACES AND WAYS TO MARKET... 170

STAY FOCUSED!.. 177

Resources 182

More Recommended Books............................. 183

About the Author 184

Dedication

To my husband, Elton and my daughters, Alyssa and Vanessa, I love you all very much.

Thanks Marie-France Scott for all your help and support. To those who encouraged me to complete this book: Derby Valentino Perez, Tina Williams and Trish Gilliam at BoldAngels.com. Thank you very much.

To Deb Lellouch thank you so very much for taking the time to edit the book for me, I really do appreciate it.

MY STORY

Wow! Congratulations you have graduated from Massage Therapy School. NOW WHAT?

Take a deep breath and pat yourself on the back you are a Massage Therapist.

Massage Therapy is an amazing and rewarding profession; it is hopefully your passion, like it is mine because otherwise it can be a challenge.

Every state or province or country has different course requirements. Please do yourself and your clients a favour and continue to upgrade your knowledge and skill with courses, especially if you have less than the 2200 hour course that is required in Ontario and BC. These courses will help fill in the knowledge gap and help you be a more effective therapist.

Massage therapy is my passion. I have been giving massage to friends and family for years and have enjoyed helping those with "knots". Little did I know how much there is to know about providing a massage, or that sometimes you shouldn't provide a massage at all, or just in certain conditions and diseases or times during flare-ups.

Generally, I would recommend taking a deep tissue, sports (again more to it than just working deeper into the tissue with your elbows), aromatherapy, pregnancy massage and any other modality that you think you would need to round off your education. I would also recommend cranial sacral therapy, neuromuscular therapy and myofascial release.

Now having said that it is important to have an understanding of these therapies but you must decide who your "ideal customer" will be and who your target market or client is (I will discuss this later) and then focus on those therapies that will enhance your knowledge and improve your skill to help that particular client or market. For example, if you will be dealing with pregnancy massage then there will be no need to take sports or deep tissue courses.

I recommend working within another clinic or health care practice for a year or two and observing all aspects of the business; not only what you would do in your own clinic someday but especially what you would not do and keep a journal of some sort. Any marketing ideas that they implement, how they treat the clients, do they try to retain the clients and how, etc. write them down in the journal because you will definitely forget some of the stuff you thought was important to note at that time. Read marketing books and perhaps take a course or two, especially if you plan to go out on your own someday.

After completing my 2 year course, I knew that I wanted to go out on my own and run a business. After graduating from University I worked for an Orthopaedic clinic for 5 years and decided to have my own practice. The decision was now: do we rent or do we buy a commercial building? We decided that after discussing rental agreements, in the area in which we wanted to locate, that the mortgage would be just as much and the landlords were unwilling to renovate. Any renovations would be our cost. We had heard that some landlords would either reduce or waive the rent for several months to compensate for the investment we would be making to beautify the place to our desire. The ones we approached did not agree; but check your area as; landlords there might be willing, especially if the economy is still depressed.

So we decided to purchase a commercial unit. Well, in Toronto, Canada, we had to have 35% down for that kind of purchase. We lived above the Clinic and I used the basement as my workshop to fabricate the Custom-Made Foot Orthotics and the rest of the space was used for storage and work-shop for my husband.

While employed at a telemarketing company I worked on slowly building my business. So we had a steady income coming in and that helped pay the bills and the mortgage. Let me tell you, there were some months we didn't know if we were going to pay all our bills, how we were going to come up with bus money and money for food as well.

I can honestly tell you that I didn't take marketing very seriously then. I didn't try to figure out my target market. I distributed some flyers around the neighbourhood, which got a few calls. I set up meetings with doctors in the area and educated them about my services (I had focused mostly on the Foot Orthotics since that was my high-ticket product and my comfort zone at the time); I did gain some business from doing this as well. We put a small ad in a local book of advertising (which was a rip off and got me no business); but the biggest return of investment was the large sign we had made which was the length of the balcony and could be seen visibly from the road. I resisted doing the sign because it cost us $400 CDN, but it paid for itself tenfold. I still had clients coming in after being in that location for 3-5 years and asking us how long we had been there because it was the first time they had seen the sign. Can you imagine if we didn't have a huge sign?

The other marketing that brought us business was the complimentary ad in the yellow pages, it was two lines with the name of the clinic address and phone number. I got a lot of response, I think, because people liked the name of the business: Head 2 Toe. It was a great location, on a main road with lots of traffic. Four bus routes were within a five minute walk of the clinic and it was a large family neighbourhood.

Let me tell you also about one of the best purchases we made. We purchased a call display unit just in case someone called and didn't feel comfortable leaving a voice mail. I would just call the number back and explain to them that they had called my Massage Therapy and Foot Orthotic clinic, Head 2 Toe, and I was wondering if I could be of any service to them. Some had the wrong number, some asked questions and said they would call back (looking for a sexual massage not therapeutic) and a few ended up being long time clients.

Just an aside, how I handled those who were trying to call for a sexual massage is.... When a male called and asked if I did a full body massage. I would respond that we can provide a full body massage depending on the area of concern; we would only undrape one area at a time and then move on to the next body part. Some would ask again, "So you do full body massage?" to which I would reply we do therapeutic massage but not sexual massage. They would either hang up or state they would call back, although they never did.

Now some men either hadn't asked the question or were less ambiguous so they had passed by my screening. They were okay until the end of the treatment and then asked if I didn't take care of them down there (at which point they looked down to their private part). I then apologized for the misunderstanding and said that I was a legitimate and professional massage therapist. They quickly paid and left.

If I had a new male client and I wasn't quite sure of him, I would have my husband walking in and out of the clinic or greet him at the clinic desk. If I had been alone, I may have had a whistle or an alarm in the room that I could press just in case.

Remember, you are in control. If you are feeling uncomfortable it is your right to ask the person to stop what is making you uncomfortable or leave the premises, and make sure you document it, just in case it goes to court. Protect yourself and your reputation!

When I first started here in Nevis, I wanted to be fair and reasonably priced for local people so they would be able to afford my treatments. So I charged $50 per hour initially. I resented it, and the local people as a whole didn't know enough about the benefits of massage or its value, so they were not my target market. I then upgraded my price. I had been charging $65 in Toronto and knew I was worth that and more. Charging a low amount gave me no way to offer a discount for my massage for special occasions or referrals rewards etc... So I increased it to $60. This year is the first year in 6 years I increased my price to $65.

Price according to your market and what you are comfortable with, you will grow into it over time. It's all about the psychology of money and knowing your worth.

SETTING UP YOUR CLINIC

Have a vision of what you want your Massage Therapy clinic to look like. The colours on the walls, the linen, the massage table, the oils, the music, etc. see it before you start to create it. Most things you will have to purchase upfront, some you will not, so figure out your budget at the beginning and work towards the end vision over time. Make it your space. It should reflect you and have a calming and welcoming feel to it.

 In the massage room, we had a soothing pale grey paint on the wall; we had my massage table, a roller chair for me and a standard chair for the client to use while going over their health history form. I would provide this complementary service as well as any postural assessment or Orthopaedic tests. I just honestly felt it was for my benefit since the more I knew, the better chance of me seeing the bigger puzzle. The pieces would fall into place for me to determine the cause of the symptoms. Taking the health history and discussing it would last from 15-30 minutes. I would also let new clients know to expect to be with me for the first treatment from 1 hour 15 minutes to 1 hour 30 minutes and why. If I hadn't seen them for 3-6 months I would just quickly go over their health history again to make sure there were no changes.

The room was lit with wall sconces with a dimmer switch, which was another great investment; there was never any worry of glare or harsh light for the client. I personally choose not to provide aromatherapy since I was seeing pregnant women and those with headaches and migraines. There were no windows or vents to remove the scent from the previous client quickly enough, so keep this in mind when you decide on your target market.

Set up a business account in order to accept credit cards and have a manual swipe machine just in case the power is down-or the bank is very busy- to process the transaction quickly enough. There are many more options now, paying online with credit card or PayPal. Check out which one has the lowest percentage rate and then determine if they meet your client's needs.

BASIC PERSONAL RULES

Hygiene

Please no nails. Your nails should be cut down to where you cannot see any white; if you are going to have longer nails, do not allow any dirt under them. I had an older therapist work on me and she did not leave a good impression because her nails were a little long and had dirt under them, her hair was long and not tied back so she kept touching it with her hands. Make sure to check the edges of your nails for possible sharpness or you could scratch your client. I worked with some therapists who had long fake nails on. To this day I am still not sure why or how they managed but they did. If you are going to paint your nails, do it with a neutral colour. Remember you are not at a fashion show; this is your office and you need to look professional.

It is imperative that you use deodorant. Be sure that it stays with you or apply more than once throughout your day. I suggest not wearing any perfume just in case someone is allergic or, at the very least, irritated by the scent.

Makeup is optional but please do not put a lot on; again be professional, be subtle and natural, use makeup only to enhance your natural beauty.

Your hair must always be tied back off your face, if long enough; at least your bangs should not be in your face. Try not to touch your hair with your hands. If you have a strand of hair that strays, then use your forearms. If you have to touch your hair with your hands, then wash them afterwards.

Do not wear dangling earrings that could touch the client while you are working over them. Try to be subtle it is not a fashion show. I also worked with therapists who wore their watches, bracelets and rings while giving a massage DO NOT DO THIS. It is highly inappropriate; it could potentially scratch the client. Germs collect under them, and they inhibit the full use of the forearm and wrist. Remember that your ideal customer pays you money to provide a great massage. Put yourself in their shoes. What would think if you walked into a clinic or spa and saw your therapist with this kind of jewelry on?

Your clothes should either be a uniform or casual t-shirt with or without a collar (although a collar is more professional). White is always most preferred, as long as the shirt is clean and has no rips, tears or stains on it. Your pants should be clean, pressed and not too tight! I am in the Caribbean and I wear long shorts in my clinic since I don't have air conditioning but when I go to a client's house, I do wear long pants. No mid-riff should be shown and the clothing should not be too tight or too loose so as to constantly brush up against the client.

If using a pump bottle try not to make too much noise. I worked with a therapist who had a lot of complaints because she just wasn't sensitive to the clients and made a lot of noise while pumping the oil from the bottle.

Cold hands, warm heart does not work in this situation If you are in a cold country or an air-conditioned room and you have cold hands or oils are cold, it can be very uncomfortable, . If it is cold, use a bottle warmer, wash hands under warm water and rub them together quickly to generate heat. Nothing is more startling than cold hands and cold oils/cream/lotions. If you know that your hands are cool or the oils are cool, then forewarn the client and let them know they will warm up with time.

Your breath should have no odour: brush your teeth so there are no food particles in between them or use mouth wash if this is something you struggle with.

Remember at the end of the day, you only get to make a first impression once, so look at yourself in the mirror and make sure you are professional in your appearance. If you are not sure, then ask a friend or loved one who will be honest with you and try not to take their recommendations personally.

LAST MINUTE CANCELLATIONS AND NO-SHOWS

This is tricky. This was something that I struggled with. For my regular clients, if they cancelled last minute it was usually a reasonable excuse and they either rebooked their appointment right then or called within a day or two.

The best way I found to decrease your chances of cancellations or no-shows was to call my clients a few days before their appointments, especially their regular monthly appointments, just to remind them. Sometimes they would rebook at that time.

If the client is new, there is nothing you can do about it in my opinion. I always get a contact number and call them 10-15 minutes after their scheduled time. For the most part they would rebook. Some said they would call back later: some did and some didn't. I had one potential new client who rebooked 3 different times. After the 3rd time I did not try to rebook her because my time and service are valuable, and if she wasn't ready to show up to an appointment then she could call me when she was ready or go elsewhere.

Have a cancellation policy posted clearly in your lobby: Please call 24 hours before appointment so you will not be charged. Also have it on your website and brochures. You may choose not to charge them, but this is a good reminder for them to value your time.

DOES MASSAGE THERAPY REALLY WORK?

Do Massage Therapy treatments actually work? I am here to tell you a very emphatic YES! I had this notion after school that massage feels good, it relaxes the person, it probably has physiological benefits that we were told about- increasing blood flow, decreasing blood pressure and stress (physical and emotional) etc. But does it REALLY WORK?

 I remember having this discussion with a colleague of mine who questioned if it did. He was working in a physiotherapy clinic and the main goals for them was billing (it seemed) and so they would only treat the body part that was in pain, not the surrounding area, even though in school we were taught to treat front and back and both sides. If someone came in with shoulder pain then that particular spot on the shoulder was worked after determining which muscles were involved. If someone came in with knee pain, then the immediate area around the knee would be worked on, not the entire hamstrings and quadriceps and calf. They got some ultrasound or a

TENS machine was used on the area, perhaps some heat and/or ice, and that was the end of the treatment. He didn't get to see and experience the true benefit of an effective treatment. Usually that person was seen a few times and that was it. Now I am not saying that all physiotherapists do this, but this was my colleague's experience.

Thankfully I had a great privilege early in my practice. Through a doctor referral, I treated a young lady who was in a severe car accident and she had many symptoms and issues so he thought Massage Therapy might work. I assessed her thoroughly by going over her health history, her ROM, passive, active movements of her neck and lower back and did some Orthopaedic tests, palpation and postural assessment. I then determined the kind of treatment and the amount of treatment she would need and sent off the paper work to the insurance company for approval.

I felt a little over my head, quite honestly, but I had faith that my training would guide me through. I even surprised myself since at the end of each treatment she was getting results, her symptoms were diminishing, she was feeling better overall and feeling more and more like herself again.

I saw her 3 times per week for the first 2 weeks and 2 times per week for the following 2 weeks and then re-assessed.

What a gift had been bestowed on me, not only getting to know this young lady and having the privilege of helping her get better; but I experienced firsthand that YES Massage Therapy DOES work. I eventually came up with a formula on treating the client one time per week for at least 4 weeks. This was usually enough time to rebalance the muscles, work out the trigger points and to release the tension and pulls of the muscles from the superficial layer to the deepest layer. This has lead to my successful quest to help people become pain free.

So please remember, do not only work the symptoms nor focus only on the body part that is in pain or discomfort, but on the entire region. This is also why a thorough health history intake is so important. We were taught to look at the person as a whole, not just a body made up of parts. Remember that sometimes the pain area is not the source of the pain. Trigger points often refer pain to other areas. Treat both front and back and bilateral sides starting always with the better side, this will give you a feel for how the better side is and also has a reflex effect on the opposite side relaxing it indirectly via the nervous system.

Remember you have the training and the knowledge and the skills that very few people have. If you are unsure about a condition or disease that a client has, do not hesitate to ask them for more information.

While working at a spa, I had a few clients with conditions I was familiar with in name but didn't know enough about it to confidently treat the client. I asked them if they had, had massage before and, if so, what did their therapists do or not do. They have lived with this condition for however long and they have become the experts on the condition, so ask some questions. If you are still unsure, err on the side of caution and either do not treat them or only apply light to moderate pressure, working superficially with slow and long strokes always going towards the heart.

MINDSET

When I first began, I wasn't completely confident in myself, my skill, or in my knowledge, and I wasn't completely confident that massage therapy would actually help get rid of people's pain. I was not confident that I would know what to do when the client came in, although I studied Massage Therapy at a school that had a great reputation and completed a medical and therapeutic 2200 hour program.

I was afraid that the clients wouldn't like the massage; but they would surprise me by paying me with a smile on their faces and thanking me for a good massage. Some would even schedule again!

If I could go back to my first year, I often think I would give all my clients a refund.

I know some of them needed to come back to see me because of postural or structural issues, muscle tightness, or pain. But I was concerned that if I asked them or suggested that they come back, they would think I was only focused on the money. Let's face it, although we are health professionals we are also working for money and our reward for a job well done is money. But this at the time hindered me from suggesting that they should come back for another appointment, I simply waited for them to book the next appointment on their own, and I let them down!

I later took a Massage Therapy marketing course and they told us that they had done a survey of their own clients and other people who have had a massage. They asked them to list the reasons they didn't go back to the same therapist for another massage.

#1 reason ----BECAUSE THEY WERE NOT ASKED NOR WAS IT SUGGESTED THAT THEY SHOULD COME BACK

#2 reason-----They didn't enjoy the massage

#3 reason-----The expense of the massage

#4 reason-----They had a specific problem and didn't feel any different after the treatment

So the take-away from this is simply telling them if you sincerely believe that another appointment would help them feel better and why. Tell them what you found during the massage and the health history intake and any assessment that you provided. MAKE SURE YOU BOOK THE APPOINTMENT BEFORE THEY LEAVE.

The reality is that we all have busy lives, and if we do not schedule something like massage in our agenda, then it will be 6 months before we get another one. I recommend they book an appointment before they leave. If they state that they do not know their schedule yet, we discuss booking an appointment anyway and we can re-schedule it if need be. But once it is in their agenda then they will usually reschedule it. If they are not comfortable with that, I ask them if they would like me to contact them, to see when would be best. If they are still hedging, then perhaps they do not want to come back, or they cannot afford it and are embarrassed to say so.

DO NOT be pushy. Be helpful and leave it at that. I also always ask the client if they need a phone call or email reminder to decrease my cancellation and no-show rate. IT works!

THE LAW OF ATTRACTION

Your business is a reflection of your thoughts, your actions and thinking behind it. "Things" are not simply happening to you. You must be practical at creating the thoughts that will serve your business.

Your subconscious mind may not be allowing abundance into your life, so be sure to try to figure out what your mental block to receiving and keeping money is, or the abundance of clients you desire will not come.

You must think of the vision of your business as the seed; it will take time before it starts to grow. It will take time before it goes from blueprint into fully realized physical form and eventually becomes your dream business.

For the plant to grow, it's not enough to plant the seed and wait for it to grow. While letting it do its work, you have your work to do, too. After you plant your seed, you must water it, and weed around it. Your job is to help create the optimal environment for it to thrive.

You must be precise with your vision of your business from the colours of the walls, to the tiles, drapes, linens, lotions, how many clients, how many days off per week or year as mentioned before. You need to get a clear concise picture in your head and write it down and revisit the vision every quarter in order to make sure you are on track, or adjust it if certain things are not working, and enhance or focus more on what is working. This is important to assess your business once a quarter, every six months or every year. So you can eliminate what is not working and focus on what is. Don't focus on how it is going to happen, just thinking about it, envisioning it, is all you need. The how will be attracted to you naturally.

The vision is the <u>seed</u> in itself; now you have to trust that the process of growth is working and believe. If you dig up the seed it will not grow; if you try to force an idea it will not work; if you push the present it will push back. You have to trust and believe the idea and give it time to germinate and grow, take root and find its resources in its own time. Try not to be impatient; it will be worth it in the end. You will get everything you envision once it is clear and concise and you know what the vision is. Being vague will only hurt the process. So put aside some quiet time to truly focus on what your dream business looks like so it will be attracted to you.

But you must work to ensure that it, the seed, has the environment and resources available to pull in what it needs.

Be purposeful, be patient and be active. Remember "God helps those who help themselves". When I first read "The Secret" by Rhonda Byrne, I felt that something was missing. I was changing my thought patterns; I was feeling more positive and uplifted but felt that I should be "doing" something more. After investigating a little more into what the authors that are referenced in the book were saying, I got the complete picture. The "doing" may be simply working on yourself, your confidence, working through your fears and overcoming them, deciding what your vision truly is and then determining what goals you want to meet and the action steps you are going to take.

According to John Assaraf, focused intention will create what you want, just like the magnifying glass burning a leaf. If your attention is unfocused then you will be less likely to reach your goal or sometimes it will take that much longer.

Be patient, it will not happen overnight. Every time I put my focus on my practice, whether that is creating another message for a flyer, adding to my Facebook page, or thinking about my next marketing plan, my business increases. FOCUS! FOCUS! FOCUS! But don't get caught up focusing on the negative. Make sure your focus is positive! There have been weeks where my appointment book is completely empty- which is not unusual for this time of the year and it can get discouraging. But by the end of the week I will have treated enough clients to pay my bills.

"If you are interested, you'll do what is convenient. If you are committed, you'll do whatever it takes" OneCoach.

 Be committed to your business, if you are not willing to be committed and focus your time and attention on growing it, then perhaps you are not meant to be a business owner, and that is okay.

When envisioning your dream business use your imagination: Dream big even if it sounds farfetched, because if you dream small then you might get what you dreamed and if you dream big you will also get what you dreamt! According to Einstein, *"Imagination is more important than knowledge."*

The biggest obstacle to most people's goals has nothing to do with any external condition or factors. It is this, according to Murray Smith, author of The Answer,*" They don't believe it will happen or that it can be done." If you don't believe it will happen, then it is most certainly guaranteed not too! Beliefs trump desires every time."*

"If you think you can do a thing or think you can't do a thing, you're right." Henry Ford

MINDSET ABOUT MONEY AND SUCCESS

I personally struggle with this all the time. When my clinic is busy I feel good and I am grateful for being busy. When business is slow, I start to get into my head thinking about not being busy and letting fear of failure and not making enough money take front and center stage. It is so important for you to work on your beliefs about money and success or you will sabotage yourself with your thoughts.

Remember negative thoughts bring negative actions and positive thoughts bring positive actions. When it is busy I get in my head that I am making more money than I need, and instead of being grateful and saving the extra money, these negative thoughts come to light and I get slow again; *the universe will make your thoughts a reality.*

If clients enter your business with problems and emerge as happy customers then you will receive the money. If you are not exploiting people and you are doing the best you can, then you deserve to be compensated and that is with money.

Money will follow as a result of achieving your main objective, which is to help people and keeping positive and grateful thoughts about being busy and therefore receiving money.

Write out some positive affirmations. They must be in the present tense as if they have already happened for example "I have 20 clients per week that pay me on time and love my massages*." In the end your thoughts determine your reality*. Positive thoughts in, positive results out; but the same is also true with negative thoughts.

"The One Minute Millionaire" by Mark Victor Hansen and Robert Allen suggests putting a thick rubber band on the left wrist and snapping it every time you have a negative thought in order to break your habit of negative talk and thinking.

Brian Tracy suggests when waking in the morning repeat 10 times, "I feel happy, I feel healthy, and I feel terrific."

Give yourself the grace, time and patience and in time you will begin to change and so will your life and business. Be in tune with how you feel and that will tell you why your thoughts are negative. Your feelings are directly related to your thoughts; take some time to figure out what your thoughts and feelings are.

Seventy by Seven is the first step to identify specific negative thought patterns you need to change. For example, "I'll never get enough clients to make enough money" can be changed to "I now have 20 clients per week, every week, which pay me on time, every time." Write the positive statement out 70 times for 7 days in a row, if you miss a day you must start from the beginning. Each time you write the positive statement write down your immediate mental response. So you write out the above statement and your thought is "No I won't." Then write that down and then the positive statement again, writing out the next thought which might be "in your dreams" and so on until you reach 70 times. Sometimes you will have no thoughts, so write "no response."   By the end you might get to a positive thought "If I work hard then I will have 20 clients per week". Try it, it works. It will not happen overnight but your mind is open to that possibility, so you will work to make it happen. It has taken me four years to get there but if you are persistent and market well you will get there!

Your negative voice will lose strength in the face of positive repetition and eventually your negative voice will be silenced and you have reprogrammed your mind.

You need to get rid of the power that your fears have over you before you can rid yourself of the fear. Once you confront the fear, it will eventually disappear.

Please read Wallace Wattles "Science of Getting Rich." It is your obligation to make lots of money so you can hire others, give back to your community with either time or money and you can live your best life. This book will help you change your mind-set about money. If you are not comfortable with making money or asking for money, then your business will not grow as it should because of your mindset due to your fears or childhood beliefs. You have to become comfortable with making money, if your desire is to create a business that makes "X" amount of money per year or you have a certain amount of clients per week or per month. If you are great at what you do then you will have to get used to receiving money.

"Compensation occurs when enough people want what you offer!" Murray Smith.

THE LAW OF COMPENSATION

What you offer (your product and/or service) is the result of your passion (hopefully) or an idea you had. It is the seed that has been planted.

"When you have a clear, concise, focused and vivid idea that translates into a commercial offering that matches up with something enough people want and want badly enough to pay then you have created compensation but just because you have what they need, they also have to <u>know about it</u>", from the book "The Answer."

"You, plus customers who want what you have to offer-----that's a business." Murray Smith

Murray states, that you must fulfill 3 things to be compensated:

1. There must be a strong enough need or desire within your target market (TM) for your product or service.
2. You must have an outstanding offering.

3. Then you must have the ability to market and sell what you have to offer.

Marketing is the engine that drives your business. It doesn't have to be aggressive or in-your-face, but subtle conversation which can lead to a client, now or in the future. It can be a flyer or a post-card or gift certificates or cards you give out with a discount posted on the back. Whatever your strategy of reaching your "ideal customer", make a plan of what you are going to do, when you are going to do it and where you can reach you target market.

I will give you an example. One night my family and I decided to go out for burgers at a local place where a lot of my TM hangs out. I met a few people I knew and they were sitting with other people. I was introduced and my client told them my profession. Questions were asked and a conversation began. My client's husband called me the next week for a treatment for his knees. That has happened every time I have gone out, not looking for business. But by taking the time and answering questions about their needs, wants and desires I can allay any fears or concerns they have and wouldn't be comfortable calling me about. This builds the Know, Like and Trust factor that Tina Williams and Trish Gilliam talk about at BoldAngels.com.

Once you have their attention then follow up with them. My biggest mistake was that I didn't follow up with information materials afterwards or call them to discuss any questions and concerns they may have had. You must put yourself out there, the more you do the better. Remember you are your business brand when you are providing a service.

When I was in the office and I was able to answer the phone, the potential client was able to ask me questions about their specific needs or concerns. Unless they were looking for a "sexual" massage, then they usually booked an appointment. Be pleasant, listen, answer their questions and then ask when they would like to book an appointment with you. They want to have a massage or they wouldn't have called. Now it is your turn to convince them they did the right thing by calling you.

You should have an outstanding offering in your marketing material that can be a discount or a gift certificate and that is what gets them to call. Then it is on you to make the reason they come back be because you are the "outstanding offering".

Don't think of marketing as selling, think of it as educating. When I talk to people I discuss the benefits of massage and what it can do for them and if they ask about me then I tell them with confidence and a smile that I can help them with their problem.

TARGET MARKET

Now where to begin…. simply determine your target market (TM) or audience. Well, that was a misleading statement because determining your TM is not simple at all.

When I opened my clinic in Toronto, I was aware that I should narrow my focus, if you are thinking everyone is my target market, you are wrong! You need to decide the group of people or the type of massage you will provide and focus on. I ignored that and wasn't as busy as I could have been. I was afraid that if I focused on one group then I would miss an opportunity and I would get less business. Sound familiar? As they say hind sight is always 20/20.

If you take nothing from this book other than determining your target market, then great! When I finally realized this my business blossomed! If you know your TM then you can direct your marketing message specifically in the language that group of people speak and in the places you think your TM frequents.

A target market or your ideal customer is a group of people that you want to treat or a technique that you want to focus on for a specific need or problem or solution.

You could work with athletes, pregnant women, cancer patients, diabetics, aroma-therapy, myofascial release, people who just want to de-stress, chair massage, in-house massage, etc. You get the point I hope. If you are not sure which category your ideal client falls under then close your eyes and focus on who would you want to be your ideal client and pick one that you would like to work with.

If you already have a business then take a good look at the type of clients you see and enjoy working with and stay focused on that type of client. If you are unsure, then collect some data from your clients either in their forms that they fill out, or ask them to fill out a survey. Survey Monkey.com is free. Check them out.

WHO IS YOUR IDEAL CLIENT?

In order to figure this out, close your eyes and create a clear vision of the type of client you want to work with. Do you prefer working with athletes, pregnant women, breast cancer clients, seniors? This vision is the core of your business. Step into their shoes and see what they look like mostly women or men, business people or stay-at-home moms? What are their needs, wants and desires, where do they hang out, where do they play, work and socialize? Do they have children, what is their financial circumstance? You want to dig deep and write this all down so you can come back to it and continue to tweak your ideal customer profile.

You then want to develop your services benefits around your ideal customer's values, meet the servicing criteria your ideal customer deems most important and then take these highest values and keep them in the back of your mind when crafting your marketing matter and sales scripts. You will talk to a stay-at-home mom very differently than to a business person. You may want to do a different type of marketing campaign for each of them. The stay-at-home mom's benefit will include time to herself, decrease in stress, peace and quiet and a break from all the demands on her. While the business person may want to also decrease in stress and peace and quiet, your message will be about relieving the stress from work and the demands on the job, whereas the stay-at-home mom will want a break from the demands of the children and the husband and the chores. You will find the mother through the mail or social platforms, blogs, etc. and the business person at his/her office or near the office perhaps via email or postcards.

For example, my ideal customer is between 45-75 years old. They are mostly very active, they are doing well financially and/or are retired, and they either live in Nevis full time or come here for 3-6 months in the winter months as a break from the cold. They have disposable income, for the most part, and value massage therapy as a part of their health and wellness, to keep them mobile and active for as long as possible. Most are not on social media and not on cell phones a great deal. So I then must find a different avenue to market to them. I send out a monthly newsletter that reminds them of me and massage and the newsletter helps build my reputation as an expert when it comes to health issues, especially pertaining to massage.

It is important to be very specific, clear and concise with age, gender, income, location, etc. The more specific you are then the Universe will work to bring that type of person to you.

In book "The Answer" check out the appendix 1 there is a form. Or you can go to www.onecoach.com/ this will show you how to determine the hot button issues of your ideal customer and what form of marketing material may be best.

Try to survey 3-12 clients you have who most fit your vision of who you want your ideal customer to be and, therefore, your target market. If you do not have clients yet, then ask people that fit that ideal customer profile and ask them some questions to help you target your message to others like them. If that does not work, then go to your local library and look up the demographic you want to make your ideal customer. The basic demographics, will give you what the ideal customer needs but not what they want.

For example, some women want a good but less expensive massage treatment, no muss, no fuss. Other women may want the "spa experience" and do not care about the money or sometimes even the quality of the massage. Some women may have a specific ache or pain and want you to help them keep mobile and free from injury and they want value and appreciate your skill and knowledge.

That is why it is important for you to also gather psychographic information of your ideal customer; information about what the ideal customer wants.

Psychographics help identify the motivation or reason they are making the purchase or why they are buying.

Demographics identifies who is buying, gives you characteristics that identify abilities, needs, interest of the customers purchasing that same product or service.

Your ultimate goal is to know, understand and deliver a solution to meet those needs, wants and desires, to provide a solution to their specific problem.

In a survey or in person, ask some questions. Why did you become a customer in the first place? Why do you do business with us? What do you like most about our business? What do you like least? Are there any other products or services you would like to see us offer? If you could have anything you wanted from a massage therapy business what would it be? What is the most frustrating or inconvenient thing about doing business with my company or any other massage therapy company?

Do not ask yes or no questions? Also ask them what frustrates them about other types of businesses—grocery stores, dry cleaners, doctor's offices, etc. All this information will help you to figure out their "hot button issues."

Once you figure out the element that frustrates your potential client or ideal customer then you can eliminate it from your business and possibly make that your "unique selling proposition", i.e. it can become what makes you different and unique from your competitors.

I used "Survey Monkey" to do my survey and was pleasantly surprised to learn that I was on track. This helped reinforce what I was already doing and kept my motivation up to continue doing what I was doing. You may be surprised to find out a thing or two about what your client's wants or needs are; it will help you reassess what you are doing and do it better, differently or stop doing some things all together.

There was a story I read about a marketing company that was hired. They went through the above process of demo- and psycho- graphics and found out that the ideal customer wasn't the men that this company was marketing to for years but women. Imagine that, a larger corporation thought they knew their customers but obviously didn't. Don't make that mistake.

You want to set yourself apart from your competition and this will help you achieve that goal.

Just explain to the clients that you are working on a project to improve your business because you want to be the best at what you do and ask if they would be willing to help and offer a small gift to them for doing the survey. Not only will you get valuable information but you will impress your clients for asking their opinions in the first place. I offered an extra 15 minutes onto their next massage as a thank you for taking the time to do the survey.

Once you complete the survey, list the five traits that seem to matter most to that customer, common attributes, needs, wants, desires, frustrations and five things that seem to matter least. Summarize the information and this will become your customer profile.

LIFETIME VALUE OF A CLIENT (LVC)

From Wikipedia, the definition is: In <u>marketing</u>, **customer lifetime value** (CLV) (or often CLTV), **lifetime customer value** (LCV), or **user lifetime value** (LTV) is a prediction of the <u>net profit</u> attributed to the entire future relationship with a customer. The prediction model can have varying levels of sophistication and accuracy.

It is also defined as the dollar value of a <u>customer</u> relationship, based on the present value of the projected future <u>cash flows</u> from the customer relationship. Customer lifetime value is an important concept in that it encourages firms to shift their focus from quarterly <u>profits</u> to the long-term health of their customer relationships. Customer lifetime value is an important number because it represents an upper limit on spending to acquire new customers.

When you are trying to figure out your marketing budget the customer lifetime value is extremely important, it will be your guide as to how much you can spend to make the marketing worthwhile. Knowing the LVC will also help you appreciate the word-of-mouth referrals and help you to also realize that if you retain a client and you treat him/her more than once then you will grow your business exponentially!!

To figure out the Clients Lifetime Value (CLV), you multiply the revenue and profit you can expect to receive from your ideal customer over the length of your relationship.

This will allow you to focus your message while marketing to your ideal customer and thereby make the most of your marketing budget. It will show you just how much money you can afford to spend on efforts to acquire each customer. If you are going to do ads in the newspaper, direct mailing, and flyers, etc. then you will at least know how much you will make from each ideal customer and how many customers will be needed to make the marketing worthwhile.

HOW TO CALCULATE LVC

Calculate typically how much the ideal customer will spend with you over a 5 year period or whatever your typical customer lifetime is on average.

Let's say you charge $60 per hour for a massage and the customer sees you 4x/year using the default lifetime of 5 years that will give you the lifetime revenue of $1200 ($60 x 4 massages per year x 5 years). Then you can subtract all the expenses generated from the revenue including total cost of goods sold, the sales and marketing costs involved in acquiring that customer.

Continuing with our example, $60 per hour and it cost $3 for lotion (approx) $2 per linen (you may want to include a portion of rent here as well). The customer purchases a total of 20x (4x/year x 5 years).Your total cost would be $100 per client over the 5 year period in expenses. If you spend $50 in sales and marketing expenses to acquire the client and another $200 over 5 years in communicating with the customer then take the total cost $350

($100 average cost per customer + $50 sales and marketing expenses to acquire the client +$200 in communicating costs with the customer) and deduct it from the $1200 (CLV). This would equal $850 (CLV $1200-expenses $350= $850).

This is an important number in order for you to make marketing decisions. If you know the CLV, you will realize that you may break even with the first client; but when you realize that you in fact make $850 over the 5 year period then you will continue to market to this ideal customer because it is worth it.

DETERMINE YOUR BUSINESS VISION

First let's define "Vision". According to the BusinessDirectory.com a vision is: An inspirational <u>description</u> of what an <u>organization</u> would like to <u>achieve</u> or <u>accomplish</u> in the mid-term or <u>long-term future</u>. It is intended to serve as a clear guide for choosing <u>current</u> and future courses of action.

So you want to have short term vision statements i.e. "In 3 months I will be seeing X amount of clients and ....." and for long term vision statements you would place a specific date on which you want this vision to be a reality. "It is 2015 and my life looks like this...."

Make sure you write down a clear, concise vision of who your client is and what your clinic room will look like and how many clients you will have per week, month, year and where you will find your TM.

You must keep your vision or the big picture in mind at all times, sometimes your vision will change or be altered, but keep thinking of the end vision.

Make sure you describe it in the present tense, as if it has already happened. Make a vision board; write it down on paper, whatever works for you. But you must have a clear, concise vision of your business. Once you have the end vision clearly set, then work backwards over the next 4 years to set your goals (see the chart below). For example, "I have 10 clients per week in 2 years from ____; they show up and gladly pay me on time."

Look at your plan and read the vision from the start and see where you want to be from 3 months, 6 months, and 9 months until you reach 4 years. Every time you identify a gap between where you are today and what is described by your business vision then identify it and your specific goal and put down what you need to do to get to your 3 month vision with your goals.

Write your vision down in the present tense in a success journal. Go over your vision the night before so your subconscious can take hold of it and the universe can set up situations to help you reach your goals and vision. Every morning rewrite the goals. This will keep you focused and give you the drive that you need to succeed. You are sending out a call to the universe and placing your order for the life and the type of business you want to bring into reality.

Because as you are sleeping your sub-conscious mind will help you attract opportunities and creative ideas for those actions to come to fruition. It will help you be self-propelled and help you take positive enthusiastic action the next day.

Think of it this way, if you were given a jigsaw puzzle and were not first shown the actual finished picture, the process would be very challenging to find which piece went where. You may still be able to achieve this, however it would take a much longer time and you may give up before the puzzle is finished.

When you can actually see and know what it is you want to create first, and then it is much easier and more fun to put the pieces together. What a feeling of accomplishment you will get when you have finished and are putting that very last puzzle piece into place. Ask yourself… What do I really want? What is my big picture? This will help you tremendously when you begin writing down your six main goals.

You can do this with all aspects of your life and you should. Financial goals—determine what you want your revenues, profits, and cash flow to be. Write it down in the present tense. "I am living a debt free life making X amount of dollars per year. I have savings and investments of X. I am financially secure." Always add an emotion to the statement to amplify the goal, words like excited, thrilled, happy, overjoyed etc…

Non-financial goals consist of the number of satisfied customers, and products you have for sale. "I am attracting 20 clients per week and I am selling X amount of products per month."

Personal goals involve the number of hours you work per week, your stress level, how much vacation time you take every year and how many personal days you take. "I work between 20-30 hours per week on my clients and my marketing. I feel great; I am happy and feel successful. I enjoy one week vacation per year and take at least one personal day per month.

Revenue Plan

TIME FRAME	NUMBER OF CLIENTS	COST PER CLIENT	WEEKLY INCOME
4 YEARS	20 PER WEEK	$70	$1400
2YEARS	10 PER WEEK	$60	$600
1 YEAR	5 PER WEEK	$60	$300
6 MONTHS	3 PER WEEK	$60	$180

3 MONTHS	2 PER WEEK	$60	$120

Once you have developed a revenue plan using the above numbers then you can multiply each by the price you will charge, and then multiply that number by how many units of each you expect to sell for a specific period. 20 massages per week x $60 = $1200 per week x 51 weeks in a year=$61,200 per year.

 If you plan to retail products then you can work that out as well. Compare it to what you are actually selling now and the amount of clients you are treating to monitor the results you are getting. Break it down into first 3 months, 6 months, 1 year, 2 years and 4 years.

To quote Napoleon Hill who wrote "Think and Grow Rich"; you must believe three things this is the first step towards getting rich. ***"There is a thinking stuff from which all things are made and it permeates, penetrates and fills the interspaces of*** *the universe. Although in substance, produces the thing that is imaged by the thought. Man can form things in his thought and by impressing his thought upon formless substance can create the things he thinks to be created. You must lay aside all the other thoughts in the universe, you dwell upon this until it is fixed in your mind and has become your habitual thought."*

Have a clear, concise vision and think about it all the time, believe it will happen and it will! Try not to let the naysayers get into your head. You can do this, I know you can.

In other words, if you can envision your dream business and life then impress those thoughts every day in your mind until it becomes your habitual thought and then the dream or your vision will become a reality. Dream big and you will achieve it; dream small and you will achieve it. So why dream small?

GOALS

I have for a long time struggled with goals and goal setting. I had a fear that if I set goals then I would be disappointed if they did not happen and I would be letting myself down. After reading many success books one of the Number 1 consistent recommendations is having and setting goals (after you have determined your vision).

"Excellence is an art won by training and habituation. We are what we repeatedly do. Excellence then, is not an act but a habit."
--Aristotle

It is not about working harder, it is about working with focus, clarity and positive intention according to Michelle Blood. It has been proven in many research studies that the people who actually write down their goals and take positive action lists do in fact achieve their goals. When you also add the power of affirmations along with clearly defined written goals and projects with a clear planned daily list, well then my friend you will become unstoppable.

What does this mean? By definition a **goal** is "the end toward which effort is directed: <u>AIM</u>".

You have a vision of what your business and life is going to look like in 3-5 years, this is your big picture. In order to have that vision come true you must break it down into goals. My goal for today is to …..Whatever activities you need to do to move closer to your vision, do it! Set out 3-6 action steps each day. According to Brian Tracy "Eat the Frog", start with the least desirable goal or action step that you want to accomplish for the day and then the others will be easier to complete.

Michelle Blood recommends: First to write down 6 main goals that you want to happen for the next year or so. Write these out every morning so they become firmly planted in your subconscious and then every evening write down a daily list of actions that will help you get closer to your goals. Do at least 3 and no more than 6 actions a day. If you do at least 3 things a day every day you will succeed!

Take action NOW, not tomorrow; don't wait for things to fall into place, don't wait for the proverbial someday! Take responsibility and take the steps you need to create the life you want right NOW!!!

Michelle suggests that if you find you are not doing all of the things on your DAILY LIST, perhaps you've put up one action step that is too big. For example, "Today I will create a website" this is an end goal, NOT an individual action. Instead, it is recommended to break down this big goal into smaller action steps like, "Buy domain name today"; for the next day, "Find web designer"; for the following day, "Get a photograph of myself looking amazing for homepage of website "; for the fourth day , "Get testimonials", "Write copy for Home page," etc... . By breaking down your goals into manageable pieces you will find that your six actions will be very easy to do. DO NOT overwhelm yourself by putting more than six items on your DAILY LIST.

Stay focused on one task until it is completed or it will take longer in the end.

MARKETING, MARKETING, MARKETING

Okay you look professional and your clinic looks beautiful and your clinic room is very inviting and relaxing. You are ready and your doors are open ready for business.

Open your doors and they will come right..... But they are not coming! Oh no, now what?

Well, if I knew then what I know now I could have been even more successful!!!!

So you have realized that opening your doors and thinking that customers will just walk in, in droves will not happen overnight. It will simply not happen. So if you are expecting to see 5-10 clients per week right off the bat, I am telling you it just will not happen right away. It will happen eventually, just not at the beginning. So if you are reading this book, as a student or you are working for someone else and wanting to start your own business, my hope is that you are getting prepared now.

You need to build a foundation, a solid foundation, learn from mine and others mistakes and successes. You must have a marketing plan; spend more time on strategy and not on the tactics. It is impossible to generate a flow of customers unless you have a strategy of how you are going to entice them to walk through your doors and not that of your competitors. Let me explain the difference between strategy and tactics.

The definition of <u>strategy</u> in the Merriam-Webster dictionary is:

> A: a careful plan or method: a clever <u>stratagem</u>
>
> B: the art of devising or employing plans or <u>stratagems</u> toward a goal.

The definition of <u>tactics</u> is:

> A: the art or skill of employing available means to accomplish an end

B: a system or mode of procedure.

In other words, strategy is the plan of action and the method you are going to use to reach your goal and the tactics are the system or action that you will put in place.

Let me ask you a very important question. **Are you interested in success or are you committed to your success?** If you are interested, then you will only do what you can do. If you are committed on the other hand you will do whatever it takes. That is a question I ask myself constantly.

Do you really want to own your own Massage Therapy practice? Will you do whatever it takes? Because if you are being honest with yourself and the answer is no, then don't do it. Not everyone is meant to be a business owner! There is a lot of hard work, headaches, and preparation in owning your own business. If you need a steady paycheck then stay where you are, at least for now or slowly build your own while working for someone else. Just don't take clients away from them for that is unethical and you wouldn't want it to happen to you.

So you have decided to be committed! Great, good choice!

MARKETING OBJECTIVE

You must know your Marketing objective.
According to Tina Williams and Trish Gilliam you
must figure out your objective. Do you want to 1.
Make more money? 2. Get more exposure for you
and your business? 3. Find traffic to go to certain
sites in order to build a list, to sell products or
services? This may change over the course of your
marketing plan. Each strategy needs to have a
marketing objective so you can plan the tactics and
the platforms of social media or flyers or contests,
etc. that you will use. Of course you can decide that
all three are your objectives, but you must decide
which one is the main objective so you can
determine what kind of campaign you are going to
create.

You must ask yourself some important questions,
"How can I achieve more profits per sale? (Retail,
gift certificates, increase your prices, decrease costs
or both).

"How can I achieve more customers and sales?"
(Optimize your customer. I book 4 appointments

within a week of each other for 4 weeks in order to meet the objective of my client, which is to become pain free and then I recommend a maintenance appointment 1 per month. You can add onto your services-wraps, scrubs, add specialty products, sell aromatherapy oils, CD's etc.)

How can I get more clients to walk through my doors (traffic)? Now the question must not only be how I can get more clients, but *how do I can get more IDEAL clients?* Optimize business marketing, referral reward program, flyers, newspaper ads, coupons, contests, Facebook ads, discounts, go to trade shows, participate in volunteer work in your neighbourhood for the local schools or hold an event during a tournament. The list is only limited by your imagination. Just make sure you have your marketing materials ready to go and your appointment book available.

You can get more exposure by creating a social media buzz around your business, get others talking about you and your business in a positive way, run a contest or hold a fundraiser for a non-profit in your area, etc.

MARKETING PROCESS

Now that you are committed to have your business become a success, you have a clear, concise vision of what the business will look like and you have determined the strategy and tactics you are going to use to meet your marketing objectives. It is time to start the sales sequence.

According to Murray Smith from "The Answer" there are typical components of a sales sequence included in these steps to:

1. Identify your ideal customer;

2. Generate leads (marketing material);

3. Quality prospects (ideal customer);

4. Present to one and interact with these prospects (hold events, or go to trade shows where your ideal customer is);

5. Convert prospects into customers;

6. Service the customers and follow up with them;

7. Up sell (with more treatments or products).

This is a rinse and repeat sequence. Once you do it with one person you can continue doing it over and over again with every client after. You may need to adjust as you learn and as your business grows.

I know what you are thinking, "I just want to help people, treat them and then they will come and refer others. I am not a sales or marketing person, it's not about the money, and it's about helping others." Does this statement sound familiar? If you do not want to market your business then business will not come to you, or it will not be as a great as it should be or as it happens all too frequently your business will not succeed.

If you do not want to "sell" yourself and your skills pay for someone else to do it. Find people who "play" at the things you have to work at or have no desire to do at all. Marketing is a MUST! You do your ideal customer a disservice by not marketing you and your business. *How else will they find you*? Think about it!

So ask yourself--- Where are you going? Analysis:

What will it take to get there? What is your plan to make money (or get more ideal customers)?

How will I accomplish that? What will your system be to increase the number of ideal customers?

Keep going through this process at least once every 3 months to make sure you are on track with what you want and where you want to be in the future.

According to Amy Roberts, "It is not the best massage therapist who gets the clients initially. It's the best marketed therapist who gets the clients."

Then it is up to you to keep the clients.

Develop a shift in your thinking: you are a business person, not just a Massage therapist.

Marketing creates your professional image; once you create your image you actually begin to create your reputation.

Marketing your business is not about telling others about what kind of massage you give or how long massage has been around. You must tell the world that you have the solution to their problem. You need to learn to *sell the results* of your massage *WIIFM-what's in it for me*?

To have a successful Massage Therapy business you must know how to sell or I like to think about it as educating your ideal customer

Amy states, "Selling is not about you but about your potential clients and their needs, wants and desires and how your product or service will fulfill those needs and provide the benefit."

So that reinforces why it is so important to figure out your ideal customer and target market so you can figure out what they want and how you are going to provide them with the solution to their specific problem.

Ask yourself, why should they visit me? What is the biggest benefit to them? What is it about me that makes me stand out from the rest? How can I show them that my Massage Therapy treatments will give the results they are looking for? What motivates my clients? What are my clients' desired end results after having a massage with me? You need to sell the benefit you will provide to them and the future outcome.

This is why advertising your qualification is not going to work when making an effort to get clients. Always ask yourself WIIFM.

You must set yourself apart from your competitors this is called strategic positioning. Then add enormous value that you give your potential clients and you will be well on your way to growing your business. I had a client who had seen several different massage therapists on the island (mostly it was about price). She had come to me because she developed a pain issue and needed more than just a feel good massage. Her friends recommended me. I asked her later what was it about me that made her keeping coming back even after we resolved the problem. Her reply was that I gave more value; I explained things to her about what she was experiencing and why; I gave her stretches to do at home; I discussed the need for ice versus heat and why and I provided a bottle of water at the end of the treatment.

In your marketing material, use guarantees, solutions-oriented advertising and add more value to the experience that people have with you. In the end your potential client will come to you for a solution to a problem.

Marketing is never about what *you* think or what you believe, *it is always about them*! Don't write like you are trying to sell something; *position yourself as the expert in your field. Sell results and benefits not your services or features!*

EFFECTIVE SALES MESSAGE

So now you have figured out who your ideal customer is and, you have figured approximately the client's lifetime value. Now it is time to put together your marketing message or copy.

Make sure your marketing copy grabs the attention of your ideal customer and engages him/her. *The message must give them enough compelling information so they can make an educated decision to use your services.* Offer a crystal clear easy-to-take next step, so they can take action to call you and book an appointment, or like you on Facebook or join your email list for your newsletter, etc.

For every 100 hundred people, the standard is to get a 1% response. If you get 5 clients that come in once or twice a year for 5 years, then you will have had a successful ad, flyer, social media outreach, etc. Remember to keep in mind the CLV.

There are many components that make up an effective sales message according to Amy:

1. Style;

2. Headlines;

3. Buying Criteria;

4. Overcoming Objections;

5. Statistics;

6. Your qualifications;

7. Testimonials;

8. Photos;

9. Price point;

10. Guarantee;

11. Call to Action.

1. Style- You should have a catchy headline and a relevant message to your ideal customer. The headlines can start with: How to… How… Why…. Which… Who else…. Wanted… If… If you…

2. Headlines- are extremely important because you only have 2 seconds to grab the attention of the person reading the copy. So use powerful, relevant, eye-catching words. This is why knowing the demographics and psychographics of your "ideal customer" is so important. Write down the ideal customers characteristics using as much detail as possible and then determine the following:

a. The No. #1 one pain that the ideal client may have (Pain can also be a hot button issue like being on time, warm hands and oil, etc.)

b. What they want to achieve from the massage. If your TM is someone with back pain, you will want to mention that you will decrease and even eliminate the pain by ....

c. List the top 5 benefits that your massage therapy brings to people. You work the muscles slowly, within the pain tolerance level of the client; you work the trigger points that maybe causing the pain, you work not just the pain point but the tissues surrounding it because the pain point maybe a referral point not the source of the pain.

d. List of special incentives that you could use to encourage more interest.

Pain or discomfort creates desire, i.e. desire for a solution and an end to pain and discomfort.

3. Buying Criteria- Each TM has its own buying criterion. That's why it is important to focus on a specific niche. Ask what are they looking for from a MT? In Sales message, describe how good it feels to be finally free of pain and what an incredible difference it will make in their lives. Then describe in detail what it is like to have the type of massage you do and tell them how you will solve their problem. *You are the solution to their problem.*

4. Overcoming Objections-Know what your potential client fears, i.e. what would stop them from having a massage? Do they have a fear of taking off their clothes and being exposed? Or do they fear wasting time and money? Or do they fear that their pain will not be alleviated?

Your goal is to try to figure out what will stop them from coming through your doors and, show them that they have nothing to worry about. This is also why it is good to be in the places your target market frequents so that in conversation those fears can be dispelled by you, so you can discover those hot button issues or objections through the survey that you will conduct. Listen closely to what your clients tell you now, they may be subtle but they will, in so many words, tell you when they have a concern.

5. Statistics-Using statistics builds authority and establishes that you know what you are talking about. Make sure you include the source of your information. Don't give only statistics, or throw them out there, but incorporate them naturally into the copy.

6. Your Qualifications-Whatever you do don't present qualifications at the beginning of the sales message. *The client doesn't care how smart you are, they just want you to solve their problem.* (Refer to where I discuss the benefits of massage not listing the features of you and your clinic.)

If they truly are interested they will check out your About Us page which should list your qualifications. But marketing copies on a flier or brochures has so very little room, so focus on the benefits, what you can do for them and again casually mention your qualifications. I can honestly tell you that most of my clients ask me briefly when they are on the table during the massage about my qualifications-and that might be only 20% of the people.

7. Testimonials-Any client testimonials indicate your value as a therapist. Testimonials build your reputation, your brand, and instantly give a potential client comfort in knowing that they can trust your skills and professionalism. I had one client tell me that she was on my website and went to the testimonials page and realized that all her friends come to me, so it was easier for her to call me.

I had a client on my table two Christmases ago and she had severe low back pain that decided to rear its ugly head while her family was here visiting. A client of mine referred her to me and I was doing cranial sacral therapy on her. One hand was on her sacrum (tail bone) and the other on her abdomen by the pubic bone. At that point I was thinking "Wow, how trusting of her friend to let me try to help alleviate her back pain by doing what I thought would help her the most." Massage is intimate; word of mouth is even more important and powerful!!! Testimonials help!

8. Photos-Your picture will speak a thousand words! Massage is a business but it is a huge thing for clients to walk into your door without knowing you. Hopefully seeing your picture will enable them to have a good sense of who you are and that will help develop the trust that is needed before they even walk through your doors. Make sure you are smiling; you lean into the camera and look professional. Remember you are the brand of your business.

9. Price Point-The price doesn't influence your client in the way you may think. If someone just wants a basic massage because they like it then price maybe the deciding factor. *If you are able to solve their problem then it usually doesn't come down to price.*

One of my clients told me recently that I am more expensive than some of the other therapists on the island. Her friends keep bugging her to see them. But her response is "Tina got rid of my back pain when no one else could so I am going to stick with her!"

10. Guarantee-Offer money back guarantee that should eliminate some of those initial fears of not getting any results. It eliminates the risk they will be taking if they have had some bad experiences in the past especially. A money back guarantee tells people you have their best interests at heart and are willing to prove it by taking the risk of working and not getting paid. I have never had anyone take me up on the offer.

The guarantee simply displays your confidence in your ability and generates a level of trust because you are not solely focusing on money but the results.

11. Call to Action-All marketing materials need to have a very clear and simple direction of what the potential client should do next. Call to make an

appointment. For a special offer, first 20 clients will receive free bottle of aromatherapy oil or 10% discount. Always have a time limit (for scarcity). This will hopefully motivate the "ideal customer" to act quickly. Also, you can keep track of when the offer begins and ends. You want people to act now!

The same customer as above read my flyer that I had posted in a grocery store. She thought that my message spoke to her but forgot to get the information down and left. She remembered half way home and turned around and came back for the information because her fear (scarcity) was that the flyer would be taken down soon!

REMEMBER that you need to earn your ideal customers trust. Positioning yourself as a person of authority will take time; it is an attitude of respect towards your knowledge and ability to solve your client's problems. It is not a given, *you must earn and nurture it; it is part of your branding and reputation.*

Amy states: "The more you value yourself in the business, the more people will value you." This will build with time, and as your confidence in your knowledge and skill grows, it will exude from you and your ideal customer will feel it too!

MARKETING COPY

We all know from grammar school that we need a beginning, middle and an end. Your marketing message is somewhat the same. Your goal and aim is to make sure that it captures the "ideal customers" attention. Keep thinking about who you are talking to: an athlete, a pregnant woman, a mother, an older person. What are their needs and wants? What problems can you solve and why would they want to see you over someone else? Also remember that *the average person's attention span is 7 seconds.* No pressure, but keep your message engaging and succinct!

You of course have to start with the ***Headline***. The headline has to be *attention getting* and is the most important part of the ad. It *"qualifies your ideal customer immediately and disqualifies those prospects who are not ideal"* according to Murray Smith from the Answer. That is why it is so important to figure out your ideal customer and target market characteristics, so you can talk to those specific customers you want to come through your door. When going through this process I decided that there were 3 markets I wanted to target. We have a medical university on the island so my message was to 20-40 year old students. My next target was to those with back pain (which I referred to above). The third was to tourists who stay in a hotel or rented house and are here to relax and de-stress. Have fun with it! Just remember to always keep your "ideal customer" in mind.

Now the ***Sub-headline*** must hold and engage the potential customer; you want them to keep them reading. We, consumers scan things quickly and if the information presented to us doesn't talk directly to us then we move on. Know what your ideal customer needs and wants and how they speak and gain information. You would speak differently to seniors versus youths, for example. The sub-headline needs to engage your prospect's attention by promising to provide vital decision-making information; it should have enough specifics to intrigue the reader to continue reading further.

Your *first line* should set up how you can resolve the hot button issue, major concern or frustration that they have.

The ***body of the copy*** is where you convince your prospect that you provide ***the*** service or sell a product that will solve their issues. Emphasize the benefits of your services specifically, not massage in general. Do not define what massage therapy is or does. By now most people know that. Again remember not to waste time reiterating your qualifications. Have that on your website, briefly mention it only if it is an important part of the message again to your ideal customer. Discuss the value you will provide for them and, differentiate yourself from your competition. Your "ideal customer" will pay a higher price if they understand the value of your service. So the body should give the greatest value with crystal clarity, but it should not be too long.

Conclude with a compelling offer to lead your ideal customer to take action. It needs to be low risk or no risk to lead them to call or email or come to your place of business or go to your Facebook page or interest page.

You need to have the big picture in view, no matter where you are in the process or what you are doing. Business is a puzzle. Know where you are and where you want to be; you need to have a clear picture of what needs to be done to bridge that gap between what is happening now and what your goal is. *Do not focus on the how;* **the how will present itself. Just** *take a step every day towards attracting that ideal customer and before you know it you will have your "dream" business.* Just make sure you are driven by passion not by mood or money!

Keep always in mind that money is a by-product of success not the mark of success. If you are genuinely passionate about what you are doing then money will follow, naturally, there is no other outcome that can happen!

You may need to work through and overcome the fear of failure or success by controlling your attitude. You can control your attitude by staying in control of the picture held in your mind.

You may experience hardship, struggle, defeat and disappointment—know that you can only be successful if you're willing to risk failure. If you are willing to take big risks then you will win big prizes in the end.

FEATURE VERSUS BENEFIT

Whether you own a spa or a clinic or work within someone else's clinic *be careful not to sell your features of the establishment but sell the benefits of the massage and what each treatment can do for them.* Tell them how you will make them feel during the massage and how they will feel after the treatment. You want to entice them to come to your establishment and keep them coming back and then bring a friend.

What is a feature versus benefit? The definition of a feature is: the structure, form or characteristic:

A. prominent part or characteristic

B. any of the properties (as voice or gender) that are characteristic of a grammatical element (as a phoneme or morpheme); *especially* one that is distinctive

In other words "hot", "red", "Swedish massage", "deep tissue", "long slow strokes" are all features but not benefits.

A benefit is:

> A. Something that promotes or enhances well-being; an advantage: *The field trip was of great benefit to the students.*
>
> B. Help; aid.

In other words, increases blood flow, decreases stress and hormone levels, increases recovery time in between events, relieves pain, helps you stay agile and active, etc.

So in all your marketing material you want to focus on the benefits not the features. I hope this clarifies the difference between the two.

DIFFERENTIATE YOURSELF FROM YOUR COMPETITION!

Think of all the things you can do to make the client's experience really sensational. You need to be able to differentiate your business and the client's experience from your competition; think about what can you do differently or better, that would make them come back to you rather than go to someone else? You can be a great massage therapist but if you are not very friendly and are not as inviting as you could be then the client may not come back to you. There are other great therapists who are friendly, positive and listen intently so be aware and give more value.

Keep asking yourself how can I improve my massage business today? What can I do to bring in more clients, whether it is adding services, adding products, air conditioning, showers, etc? What actions can I take to increase the word of mouth rate? It may not have anything to do with your massage. It might be a little thing about their experience with you from the time they walk into the waiting room until they get back into their car. It could be perhaps as simple as a complimentary bottle of water or educating the client on some homecare stretches or ice and heat applications, when to use them and why, discussing nutrition and exercise and so much more.

If they mention something they like, then perhaps (if not too expensive) get that for them the next time they come in. Try to remember some of your conversation from the previous session and ask them some questions; this will show that you were listening and that you are genuinely interested in them and what they had to say and it builds a relationship.

Sometimes my clients have other issues with their bodies that massage cannot necessarily help directly, so I will do some research and email them with information or products that I can recommend.

I read somewhere that in the cold climates some therapists are putting on feet warmers and hand warmers during the treatment, warm towels on the bed, soft music or specific music they would prefer, offering a bottle of essential oils, gift card, information booklets, or foot balm, or hand cream. The sky's the limit, so be creative. ***Give the client a reason to talk to others about what you did for them***. It will be the best form of marketing you will ever do!

I have done client appreciation weeks for my existing clients, offering them a discount for a certain week (one that is usually slow). This will make them feel appreciated and special and they may tell their friends and family but if nothing else it creates good will.

I have read that someone suggested sending a thank you card to new clients for coming with a message about looking forward to meeting them again and helping them with…. I personally email or call all new clients a few days later thanking them for choosing me to help them solve their particular problem, then ask them how they felt after the treatment. This does two things; it allows me to answer any questions or concerns they may have and it shows that I care.

I also call or email clients who refer other people to me to thank them for the referral. You can send or give them a small gift from a body shop, a gift voucher from you, a gift voucher from a book store, box of chocolates, flowers, 2 movie tickets, or a relaxation CD. If my clients refer 3 or more people to me they get a 30min free massage.

Now you might be thinking, "Wow, I am barely making any money as it is, how can I afford to pay for something extra?" Remember two things: it is the thought that counts; they will probably go tell their friends and also may be even more motivated to be your advocate and promote your business. Also think of the client lifetime value and that gift will seem too small a reward for a client helping you to grow your business.

YOUR REPUTATION

It is important to create a professional and positive reputation. Your reputation starts with an image. The image of your service and professionalism will create your reputation. It is up to you to nurture it and protect it. Everything you do- especially if you live in a small town, or even when you post on-line- reflects you and your business reputation. Be mindful of this!

If you think about it, from your client's, if you have negative beliefs about a business would you patronize that business? Probably not! I know I wouldn't. If you started with a less-than-stellar reputation, then try to create a new belief system for yourself and then the business. You will have to work longer and harder to change the opinions out there, but it can be done. So save yourself a lot of work and aggravation and do things right in the first place.

We are the business! Your marketing and attitude have to be good, and it is one of the core ways to attract clients and then keep them coming back and referring others to you. Speak as if you are only talking to one person (target market); they will feel like you understand them perfectly and that you are the only one with the answer. I did a flyer campaign and I targeted people with back and neck pain, one of the clients who came to me because of the flyer said, "I read your flyer, I had back pain and it was as if you were talking to me, I just knew you could help me, although I have been to other Massage Therapists on the island."

Later she told me that she never thought that back pain could be "cured"; she thought that she would "have to live with it." So now she tells everyone she knows that has back pain that she is pain free and refers them to me.

You must portray a highly positive image; a photo of you is a great way to do this, according to Amy, in your marketing materials from your flyer to your business card. You must project good energy, confidence, and commitment. Your message must match the picture you have created. The more positive expression you have the more you will attract clients.

Since Massage Therapy is about trusting the therapist to do a good job and solving their problem, they will want to see who you are, so they can get a sense of your character and trustworthiness. I have my picture on my clinics Facebook page, LinkedIn, Pinterest page. If you have a Twitter or YouTube page then they must see you in a professional, positive light. Think about it. If you never had a massage before and you saw a flyer or a website or a Facebook page would you chose the business with a smiling, trustworthy, professional picture of the therapist? Or one with a lot of words and interesting pictures?

Your marketing should tell your potential client what type of therapist you are, type of person you are, what your attitude is towards them, how much they can trust you and how happy you are, how much you value their business and how willing you are to help them and that you are prepared to provide them with extra special treatment.

BRANDING YOU AND YOUR BUSINESS

According to the Business Dictionary, Branding is the <u>process</u> involved in creating a unique name and <u>image</u> for a <u>product</u> or service in the <u>consumers'</u> mind, mainly through <u>advertising campaigns</u> with a <u>consistent</u> theme. Branding <u>aims</u> to <u>establish</u> a <u>significant</u> and differentiated presence in the <u>market</u> that <u>attracts</u> and <u>retains</u> loyal <u>customers</u>.

In the beginning do as much marketing as possible that suits your budget. Use all free resources in social media marketing, talk to people and add flyers, create a brochure, use the same picture in all of your material, same colours and the best 3 words that best describe you and your business or your USP (unique selling proposition).

By Definition: A Unique Selling Proposition can be summarized in one short sentence. Why buy yours instead of the others?

In more detail, the Unique Selling Proposition (USP for short) is what sets your products and/or services apart from your competitors. The catch is that the proposition must offer your potential customers a specific benefit that they see as attractive.

Expressed as a single sentence that summarizes the essence of your business, the Unique Selling Proposition serves as the theme of your marketing.

A Unique Selling Proposition is an especially critical marketing tool for small businesses that are forced to compete with both other small businesses and larger retail chains.

To create a Unique Selling Proposition, ask yourself, "What is it that my product or service offers that my competitors' products or services don't offer?"

Then ask yourself what specific benefit this provides your customers. For example Hallmark: When you care enough to send the very best.

Subway: Subs with less than 6 grams of fat. By <u>Susan Ward</u>, About.com Guide

Your branding and reputation go hand in hand. Make sure all your marketing is consistent, clear and professional. There should be a general theme that goes through all your materials using the above colours and the USP.

Be prepared from time to time to get negative feedback and try to learn from the client why they didn't like the treatment or whatever the complaint may be. Also this is an opportunity to ask some questions. If they felt so good afterwards maybe they started doing things they shouldn't have done yet. It is important because you may be able to explain why they felt like that and it will allow you to persuade them to come back.

Remember in today's world we all want quick fixes and we are sometimes are not patient enough to allow things to work. At the very least you will be able to show that you care even though things may not have worked out with them and they may not say negative things about you or they will speak less negatively about you. You may be able at the very least, be able to change what happened with another client in the future if the complaint is something within your control, like being on time.

BUSINESS CARDS

Your business cards are a point of contact, name, number, email, website, logo/USP perhaps your picture but this is usually not a marketing tool. But if you add a dynamic QR code it most certainly can be. The code when scanned by a smart phone can then lead the potential client to a mobile site, a testimonial, a welcome video, and your website, to a coupon or a contest, or a discount… whatever you want.

Amy Roberts, who wrote, "Ignite Your Massage Therapy Business Marketing Secrets for Massage Therapists," recommends using a picture of yourself, looking friendly, smiling, with a slight head tilt and leaning into the camera which gives you an approachable look. Just a headshot wearing professional massage clothing or a uniform is what you want. Personally I have never used my own picture I have used a graphic my husband designed to accentuate my USP for the first business and a piece of the design that was on my brochure for the second one.

You can use your business cards to give to existing clients to give to friends and family with perhaps a message with a special discount for them on the back. If the client has really enjoyed your treatment perhaps ask them to take some of your cards and ask if they would be willing to refer you to their friends and family. If they have your information in their wallet it will be easier for them to promote you by handing out your card instead of having to remembering your contact information or remember to email or call someone later.

WEBSITES

Here are some basic pointers on websites. Firstly, you must decide your objective for the site. Will it be a marketing tool, collecting addresses to send them to an offer or newsletter or a blog? Do you want to give them educational information or discuss you and your services? Or will it be a resource for the client or to get new business?

My website is simply to give further credibility; they can check out my mission, learn more about me, my services provided and my hours and price list and read the testimonials from my clients. Honestly though the only page on my site that gets looked regularly is my home page for the most part. Some people will look further but not a high percentage.

So make your home page the most important message. Remember to talk about the hot button issues or fears or needs of your "ideal customer" and let them know that you can help them and what the benefit of them coming to you is. (Refer back to

Effective Sales Message and Marketing Copy sections of the book.) Be consistent in your message. If you have a comment section or opt in page reply to a client within 24 hours.

Keep the information concise, relevant and specific to your ideal customer's needs (remember message to your target market).

Having a domain with your name in it can work better because you ARE the business. That also means that your company name should be the same or similar as the domain name. Since I live in a small island and I had a reputation already in the community I named my business Tina's Clinic. This may not matter if you are in a large city. My clinic name in Toronto was Head 2 Toe and I am sure that the name got me a few phone calls.

You can have someone make your website, or you can use a company that has a template for you to follow and you can create it. Make sure that before you do any print material and name your company officially to search the domain names at namecheap.com. It may not be available in the form you want it so you may have to play with it. Also if you have to register the business then check with the registrar first to make sure that the name is available and then the domain name.

You can get a personalized email address (leads to more credibility), or Gmail or yahoo addresses work as well.

SOCIAL MEDIA MARKETING

Build it and they will come! We all know that is not true, just like creating your business and opening your doors will not bring in a ton of clients. If you put up a Facebook page, Twitter page, LinkedIn profile or Pinterest page they will not automatically bring in clients or fans, nor will you engage a community and create a conversation. As Tina Williams says, *"Build a community around your business, and your community will build your business around you."*

You have to have a plan; just like you planned who your target market and ideal customers are and how and where you were going to market to them, you need a social media marketing campaign plan too.

"Those who fail to plan, plan to fail."

You have to determine what the purpose of creating the pages are and why you are using social media in the first place. Some platforms may work better than others; again this is determined by your target market. For the sake of argument, I am going to assume that the reason you create these pages and use these platforms is to get more business! Once you determine your demographics of the "ideal customer" then you can decide what platform to use or not to use and what they are looking for.

Please be careful of what you post on the internet especially, social media. Now employers are looking at these pages to get a feel for you and the type of person you are outside of work. You don't want a potential customer seeing that you have been negative about another customer or that you make inappropriate comments. Remember people are watching even though you don't think they are. Negative comments should never be made. Tell the truth or don't say anything at all. I also don't recommend playing games, and if you do, make sure they are off hours from the work day. Do not complain about anyone you work with. Email your friend if you need to discuss a situation. You cannot take back what you have posted on social media.

People will develop a relationship with you through these pages building trust and social proof of your brand and reputation. Be conscious of everything you post, think of your reputation and BRANDING! There are many social media platforms that you can use to grow your business and educate your ideal customer. Next, I am going to discuss the main ones that will help expose you and your business brand.

LINKEDIN
It is important to set up a LinkedIn profile. LinkedIn is a very professional platform for you to expose your business and build your reputation and brand. Try to connect to people in your community and target market. Then you can join groups within that market and perhaps even create a group to steer the conversation. The entire purpose is to show that you are the expert in your field and to show your professionalism.

Most of you are doing business within a short distance of your location. Find the search bar at the top and type in the ideal customer with the town or city name behind it and all your first and second connections will come up. You could invite them to be a part of your connections and introduce yourself to them. People would like to work with people they know; this is your foot in the door.

If your target markets are athletes and you live in Tampa Bay then type that in and see who comes up. You could also click on the groups section and look for your target market there. Once you are in the group you can add to the conversation about what they are talking about. Only focus on issues that are important and relevant to them and educate them on how massage can help. Answer questions and your profile will build and establish you as an expert within that group.

I have found it great for discussions amongst other therapists on how to treat certain conditions or situations, to get some marketing information, to get some advice of how to handle a particular client, to discuss challenging clients and how to handle them, etc. In my opinion this is the only social media platform that you can rant about a client or a business situation but still be careful, don't name the person just discuss the situation.

LinkedIn groups are very educational and informative and it is amongst your peers. You may or may not get clients from it but it is a great resource. In my social media business, answering questions can show my knowledge and expertise and it will show my level of influence. If you ask a question and that question gets a lot of input you will be deemed an influencer for that time frame. If you are looking to teach or to work in a particular demographic then it is good to source those places.

Did you know May 5, 2010 facts are that people visit the website in 62% of the cases from home (38% at work)? Roughly 1% of the LinkedIn addicts are responsible for a staggering 34% of all visits! 62% are passers-by and responsible for 18% of visits. The audience demographics for LinkedIn.com, relative to the general internet population, looks like this:

LinkedIn Graph

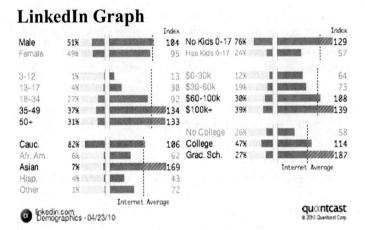

Posted by Jacco Valkenburg
http://www.globalrecruitinggroundtable.com

For LinkedIn it is important to build your "connections", the more people you have within your connections then the more people you expose your business to. You can have 1st, 2nd and 3rd connections.

Make sure to again have a great picture of yourself. I will not connect with people without a picture or a cartoon. Fill out your entire profile; this is your first impression for someone looking to connect with you.

Start with your friends and then add to your list of connections. Ask them to join your professional network. You can send them a basic invitation but I would recommend sending them a personalized invitation. Once you click on connect you will be prompted to tell LinkedIn how you know them and then just below that, you can add a "personal invitation". It has limited characters so be concise.

Make it a goal to connect with at least five people every day and before long you will have several hundred connections and potential clients.

Start endorsing other's that you know and they will return the favour; this builds credibility within your field. This is also why it is important to fill out your profile thoroughly.

Unless you are looking to be hired by someone, this is not meant to be your resume. You want your ideal customer to read your summary and feel like you are speaking to them directly (refer back to marketing copy and message.)

You can have a personal account and also a business account. Go to your profile then go to interests. The drop box will have "companies" click on this and then on the top right side will say "add a company". You must have a specific company email not a gmail, for example, @thatbusinessname.com.

If you are unsure on how to fill out your profile page, to attract customers, or gain professional opportunities then message me http://www.linkedin.com/in/tinaahull/ . I will help you out.

PINTEREST

Pinterest is the newest social media platform on the block and is mostly about posting pictures. Recently, you can have a business account separate from your personal account which I highly recommend. Once you set up your business account, take pictures along the way of different events, functions, milestones and charity work you participate in or sponsor and pin them on your boards.

Pinterest is more of a marketing tool to expose your business and build trust with pictures. Determine how you are going to set up your boards. Make a plan of things you want to share with potential ideal customers.

Pinterest demographics are women mostly between the ages of 25-55. Since you have determined your target market then you can build boards that would be of interest to them. Remember pictures tell a thousand words so make them memorable and fun but always professional. For your business page make it all business oriented though. For example, if you are targeting pregnant women you could have different boards on clothing, names, girls, boys, massage and pregnancy, post partum information, perhaps room decorations, stores that cater to pregnant women and babies. You could also have a board on babies, toddlers etc...

Make sure you fill in your profile well. If you have an email, Facebook page, website, etc. put it into your profile so you can be found.

Use hash tags (#) for specific categories or interests so that anyone looking for information within that category will be exposed to you and your business.

When you sign up on the lower right side, there will be a tab for businesses click on that and get started. You can also have a personal page as well but on this platform you don't have to have a personal page to have a business page unlike Facebook.

There are some fun things you can do with Pinterest. If you have products that you are selling you can link a website to your page and have a link within the picture, so if people are interested they can purchase the product. If you are holding a contest you can link your Facebook and Pinterest pages together and ask people to share the information with their friends and family. Check out contests in the business section under the "brand guidelines," make sure you read the rules first. If you have a website you can get a link on Pinterest to invite your followers to pin what they found on your website to Pinterest (under widget builder.) You will also find a "pin it button" section that you can copy the script or have your web designer do it and add it to your website or blog post.

Check out the tab of "success stories" to get examples. As Tina Williams always says "success leaves clues." You obviously cannot copy everything someone else is doing but you can design around with the same principles in mind, figure out what you like about the different boards and mimic what is working for them onto your boards.

Once you have decided on the boards then you just pin the pictures you find onto the different boards you have named. You can have a link to your business on some of the pictures along the way.

When you have logged into Pinterest then go to the left of the page. Type in the search what category that you are looking for i.e. "babies", a group of pictures will come up then you start pinning them to your boards.

You can also hover over the icon that has 3 horizontal lines and click on "sports" and then look for the pictures you would like to pin to your board. When you are at events, you can post pictures of your day directly into Pinterest. Check out some other boards and use them as a guideline.

With Pinterest you can post as many times as you like. It goes into a feed but people will not get an email telling you that people posted- something unlike other platforms. You will get an email letting you know that someone pinned one of your pins though.

Keep in mind you can also do video on Pinterest as well, to build exposure for your business and promote an upcoming event.

Most of all have fun and create an interconnection between the social media platforms.

Check out this link on how to use Pinterest as a marketing tool.
http://www.mdgadvertising.com/blog/wp-

content/uploads/2012/02/infographic-marketers-guide-to-pinterest.png

FACEBOOK

Facebook is the largest social media platform out there. You must set up your personal page in order to have a business page. Make sure that the pictures tell a story; your picture should be either on the cover or the profile picture to build trust.

Remember your target market and then create the cover picture with them in mind. My clients are older, mostly women in their senior years so I have a picture of an older woman with back pain, me with a client and a woman looking healthy and joyful. https://www.facebook.com/tinasclinic

If you are working with athletes then you will want to have a various sports; if you work with a specific sport then have only pictures of it. You get the point I am sure. Just make sure not to use anyone else's picture without permission. I used http://www.fotolia.com and my own picture to create my cover page. You can set it up on power point or Pic Monkey which will allow you to modify the pictures and create collages and it is free.

Facebook changes their terms of service quite frequently to many people's dismay. As of today, June 6th, you are allowed to put a web link and contact information within your cover page as long as it is no more than 20% text. So be aware of this is if you are creating your own page.

My ideal customer is generally not on Facebook so my objective is to educate those that are paying attention about why they should get a massage, the different conditions, diseases and injuries that massage can help with. I discuss nutritional information and overall wellness important to my TM for those who are paying attention. My content is mostly from other people or I add informational tips and reminders. Just make sure you give the credit to the person that created the information in the first place.

You can have tabs on Facebook for people to join your list, to receive your newsletter or to be contacted for a contest or special events or get a discount for liking your page or being active on your page. You can connect a link from Pinterest so if people are interested they can link through to check that page, also with Twitter. You can share about any charity or community work you do to help build your brand.

You can do polls, ask questions, have fun and be interesting. Talk about the things that your community wants to hear about (know your TM), promote other businesses and other people. Thank your customers that are recommending you on Facebook and encourage your clients to go to your page and post a comment. You can highlight a post or pin it to the top of the page which will stay for 7 days.

You need to optimize and customize your business page as much as possible. To customize your business I mean to make sure that you have a profile and cover page that talk to your target audience, have a call to action (book an appointment now, call us at 123-4567). Fill out your profile section thoroughly. When I talk about optimizing it, I am talking about SEO, search engine optimization. In the about section, on both pictures you need to add as many links and keywords pertaining to your business as possible, so your ideal customer can find you and so can Google.

I would recommend not posting more than 3 times per day 3 times per week or 1 time per day every day. It depends on your objective though. Are you trying to promote something that is coming soon or are you educating your community about something or are you just reaching out and reminding people you are still around?

The most important part of Facebook is to be real, add good content and create a buzz!

You can get more tips and tricks of marketing at https://www.facebook.com/massageandmarketing and if you have any to share with us you can add some as well.

TWITTER

Twitter can be quite valuable from a marketing point of view for events that you will be sponsoring or holding. You would use twitter to promote the event to get more people to come or just to let your community know that you are involved. You can have twitter parties about a particular subject that your target market is interested in. This is again builds your brand and reputation as the expert.

You can have personal accounts and business accounts on twitter. You use 120 characters out of the 140 given so others can retweet your comments. Make it interesting; quotes, food for thought, some basic tips about health and wellness. Pay attention to what others are doing and see what is getting a lot of following or buzz.

If you retail products then you can add a link every once in a while but do not overdo it; make it part of the conversation.

Send people from your Twitter account to your Pinterest account to your Facebook account to your LinkedIn account to your website.

You can have a contest on Facebook. Then you would use Twitter and Pinterest to drive traffic to your Facebook page and advertise it on LinkedIn for marketing, for example. There are endless things you can do to create a buzz about your business, you just have to creative and think outside the box.

For Twitter, because the feeds are so fluid and rapidly moving, you could post a comment at least 1-3 times per day. You could do one in the morning, then in afternoon and then the evening. Again keep in mind your TM. Test what times your ideal customer is responding to and then follow the patterns.

You can tweet me at @marketmassage to follow along as I continue to give out some tips and tricks of marketing.

QR CODES/MOBILE SITE/TEXT MESSAGING

QR codes are quick response codes that look like a scan code. You can put QR codes on all your print material. Persons can scan the code using a QR reader on their smart phones. Once they scan the code you can direct that person to whatever you want them to be directed to. You can have them scan the code and send them to a coupon, or a special, or a new product, or to your website, or to your mobile site, or to a place to book an appointment or to your price list etc.

At one point QR codes were stagnant so if you changed the special you were pointing the code to; you had to completely reprint all your materials again. Now they have a system whereby you can change the direction of the code by the minute, week, month and you use the same code (no reprinting all new material so you reduce your marketing costs and save the trees too!).

You can use it to send them to a text campaign. If you scan this and text, to this number you can win, or you can send them to receive a discount. People love to be interactive and entertained, so give them a reason to scan the code. Make it worth their while and give them again something to talk about. Make sure though, that you don't send them somewhere they would not be expecting to go to. Also make sure you scan the code before you put it onto your print material, making sure it works.

At some point you may want to invest in a mobile site since mobile is growing substantially. More people have cell phones worldwide these days.

The increase in the number of mobile cell phones in the world has been impressive. The graph on the website below shows subscriber growth between 2005 and early 2013, according to ITU figures. The 6.8 billion subscribers are approaching the 7.1 billion world population. The graph shows that as world mobile-cellular penetration approaches 100%, market saturation grows and the growth rate decreases. According to http://www.internetworldstats.com/mobile.htm

To see more about the growth of mobile usage visit this link http://www.smartinsights.com/mobile-marketing/mobile-marketing-analytics/mobile-marketing-statistics/

See an example below of a QR Code. I set this one up as a loop it will change after 1 min to a different post. Download your free QR code scanner on your Smartphone. It will go to a basic coupon and then 1 minute later to a different page, 1 minute later scan it again and you will be sent to my Facebook page and then finally my LinkedIn page.

I am just showing you what can be done. You can schedule something around every 3 days, 1 per week, 1 per month, whenever you would like.

QR Code for Tina's Clinic

PARETO'S LAW OR 80/20 RULE

Pareto's Law states, 80% of revenue is generated by approximately 20% of your customers. Clients that love what you do for them will tell others and will keep referring others to you. There is no more powerful marketing than positive word of mouth from a very satisfied customer.

So now you have to figure out how you are going to create that positive word of mouth. You do this by attracting the right client in the first place. *Your ideal client is the one who really wants what you have to offer, they don't just use your products, and they love your services and feel they couldn't live without them.*

Once you identify your ideal client you'll find you'll be working less and earning more –a great deal more.

So go out of your way to protect the customers you have, treat them with respect and listen to them. Keep them coming back and create some interest in your business in order to give people something to talk about in a positive way; *if it is not worth talking about then it is not worth doing,* according to Andy Sernovitz.

You must find the customers that will talk about you. Give them a reason to talk about you (a special offer, great service, a new feature, etc.), help them spread the word faster and farther (give them handouts, samples, coupons, have an online discussion, etc.), join the conversation by replying back to the feedback, and try to keep track of what is making them talk and who is doing the talking.

You must make it really simple for them to spread the word. Put a "tell a friend" link on every page, send a cool email with a link that everyone will want to send along, customize and give or sell retail products with your business name and contact information as a reminder to them and to promote your business while they are using your product.

Ask yourself when your customer walks out the door. What have I given them to talk about? How will they remember to tell their friends? Could I have made it easier for them to talk to more people about me? Was anything about their experience remarkable?

Try as many little things as you can until you find ones that people start talking about. *People love you and your company so they talk about you; they want to feel good and want to belong to a group so give them a reason to be a part of your "team" and help you spread the word about you, your business and product.*

WORD-OF-MOUTH MARKETING

Word of Mouth (WOM) is the best form of marketing and it is free. *It is the most genuine form of advertising, it gives you credibility and means that you are effective, worthwhile and a good value for the money.* Word of mouth marketing is great when you already have customers, but a real challenge is when you don't. Read:" Word of Mouth Marketing: How Smart Companies Get People Talking" by Andy Sernovitz, Seth Godin and Guy Kawasaki

That of course works both ways; negative experiences can spread like wildfire and never be taken back. *It takes several times longer to re-build a positive reputation and brand, than to have it torn down by a negative experience*. So be careful and handle negative experiences professionally. Don't make it personal and try to rectify the complaint, try to turn the negative experience into your best customer that will be part of your positive WOM team.

After you have a client and they loved your treatment and are coming back again then you want them to part of your word of mouth team. You need to nurture that relationship and encourage them to help you build your business! Ask them either after the appointment or in a welcome email if they would be so kind as to let their friends and family know. Most people would feel honored to be asked to spread the word about your business.

You could write them a letter telling the new client how you value them and would appreciate those referring clients or recommending you to friends. A client you have seen for a while you could write them telling them how you appreciate their loyalty and that you would love to have more clients like them in your business. Offer them a special deal if they refer clients to you. I have offered a complimentary half hour massage for every 3 clients that are referred and book with me. You can offer them anything, i.e. something they would be impressed with so they cannot refuse. This, too, will create a buzz around your business and they will talk about you anyway.

You could create a VIP or a gold customer membership so they get informed of all the up-coming events, specials and discounts before everyone else. You get the picture: focus more on the clients you already have and your business will grow exponentially! *It is harder to gain a new client than to keep one you already have happy (remember the 80/20 rule).*

Send special offers to them on their birthday; send a card with a voucher or lotion or a favourite CD etc. Your goal here is to impress them.

Remember Mother's Day and Father's Day, send them a card or a special offer, call them personally. I usually have an offer at this time and send them an email celebrating the day. Did you know that *referrals generate 70% new customers in most businesses!* Once you have clients then reward them and keep them talking about you and your business.

When I first started in Nevis, I had massaged at a 10K run event. It was at the end of the season of my ideal customer so I didn't get any clients from the event that day. But one of them recommended me to her friend who lives here full time-and not only was she my first client but she has been my biggest advocate and recommends me all the time.

According to Jay Abraham *WOM customers spend more each purchase, buy more often, refer more customers, and trust your recommendations more.* So that begs the question, why more businesses don't spend more time and money on customers that refer others and work harder to retain the customers they already have?

I worked with a Chiropractor office, and although they did quite well, they could have been doing so much better. They would treat the client and help them out of pain but then would not follow up on them or recommend monthly maintenance appointments. Everyone is different, but in my experience, depending on the client and their activity level, they need to come back at least once a month. Some came every 6 weeks and others came every 3 weeks. You will have to work with your client to judge what is best for them.

Your goal should be to love your ideal customer, place your focus on the people not the profit. Try creating an amazing experience; little extra touches like feet and oil warmers during the winter can make a massage experience amazing.

Give them incentives for giving you referrals. Discounts, and free gifts and a thank you note via email or mail will show your appreciation.

Remind your clients that you are still looking for new clients and that you would appreciate it very much if they could help you spread the word.

Ask them after they feel great from the massage you just gave them and because you delivered so much or have gone beyond what they expected. If you are not comfortable with doing this in person then write or email them.

WOM marketing is the easiest and cheapest way to grow your business profitably, according to Martin Russel International Pty. Ltd. 2004.

It takes less money to keep a client you already have then to try to earn a new client, so keep this in mind. WOM is free advertising and you will get better results than from traditional marketing. WOM supports your ads and message and spreads them around.

There are more customer leads and free prospects that can come in every day from personal referrals. It also reduces your customer service cost and builds a stronger brand, which adds up to a healthy and positive reputation, according to Murray Smith.

The Net impact of WOM marketing is more business, higher return on investment and lower costs overall. Satisfied customers who spread WOM are the most powerful assets you have so treat them like gold.

Sometimes your clients are not comfortable talking to others so be selective in who you ask and how you ask. Create a buzz around your business and they will not be able to help it, they will talk about you. Just make sure that it is a *positive buzz*.

Exceeding their expectations will generate momentum in the word of mouth referrals.

NETWORKING

Networking is another way to market you and your business. You can gain business by simply having a conversation about what you do. You need to network so people can see you as genuine in promotion of your Massage Therapy business and they can see your energy and feel your passion and excitement in your eyes about your business and chosen profession.

Go to different functions where other types of therapists or anyone else who could refer to your business are hanging out and socializing. *Remember you ARE the business!* Have a casual conversation, answer questions asked of you, but don't sell your business.

I worked New Year's Eve at a friend's restaurant that my ideal customer also frequents. By doing that I was asked by 3 different people for my card and I gained 3 new clients. It is about putting yourself out into the world. This was an unexpected return for helping out a friend.

So for example, if your TM is pregnant women you could visit your local retail store and you could have their cards in your clinic and then ask if you could have your cards in their store. Perhaps, offer the store owner a free 30min massage. Telling one person about your business could have a ripple effect because they may tell others even if they do not use your services.

Networking is about having a conversation with another person who may be able to recommend clients to you. Focus on them, their business and eventually the conversation will come around to you and your business. Try to exchange business cards. Let them know that you would be interested in referring clients to them potentially and perhaps they would like to do the same and if they are in agreement, come up with a way to best help each other.

Make sure that you work with a professional whose customers would need your services and perhaps send an email or letter or some brochures about the benefits of massage for their customers. For example, a dentist, you could discuss how you work with TMJ clients and that massage can help alleviate the facial and TMJ muscles so they will be in less pain etc. Now be aware that some people might feel threatened, because if you do your job too well they might think they will lose a client or make less money. Personally, I am always thinking of the betterment of my client, so referring them to someone who will help make things better is a good thing, I believe that will strengthen their trust in me and karma will allow it to work itself out.

Join networking groups. In Toronto, I joined a breakfast group and although I didn't get any business out of it, I learned a great deal. I wasn't very consistent in going so perhaps try one in your immediate area or start one and see where it goes, especially if your ideal customers are executives.

Meet up groups, chamber of commerce's and wellness fairs are all great places to network with professionals and like minded entrepreneurs. Perhaps you would be asked to do a talk on the benefits of massage in the work place, you just never know.

STRATEGIC PLANNING

You must plan to create an angle in your marketing that is different and stands out from your competition. Strategic planning involves knowing not only who you are marketing to, but where they are, what they want and how you can give them it to them in order to get your message across.

Take your time and make a plan of what will be the most cost effective way to reach your ideal customer. No one else is going to market for you, unless you pay them.

The traditional way of marketing is: ME = Product or Service =Money= Client Needs and Benefits

Now that has changed to:

Clients Needs and Benefits=Product or Service=ME=Money

Most Massage Therapists believe that if they tell potential clients about themselves and their skills that this will lead to lots of clients and then they will cater to their clients' needs. You must keep in mind at all times that your potential client wants a solution to their problem. Amy put it in an acronym WHAM

*W*hat and

*H*ow does this

*A*ffect

*M*e?

This comes back to the benefits versus the features of your business (refer to that section of the book to clarify my point). Ask yourself constantly, What and How does (what you and your business offer) Affect Me (the ideal customers)? How will they benefit from you and your services? If you keep this in mind at all times you will succeed!

SOME PLACES AND WAYS TO MARKET

Best places to network are fairs, festivals, exhibitions, business and service exposures or demo breakfasts or lunch groups and meet-up groups. Hand out your business cards/brochures, get phone numbers and follow up with a phone call at any event. If it is a social event, then wait to be asked for a card before giving them one.

When working at an event you can provide massage $15 for 10-15 minutes for example at a booth and try to book appointments on the spot and offer a discount for doing so. Ask some of the people running their own booths if they would like a free massage to get the ball rolling. Also discuss having them to refer their customers to you in the future.

Make a profile of the type of person who would actually refer a client to you. Think about other services in the community your massage clients may use and approach them about doing some joint marketing or having each other's cards at the front desk. I personally offered a complimentary 30 min massage to some movers and shakers in my community so they can spread the word.

Try to figure out the professionals that your target market will use in your immediate area like podiatrist, physical therapists, osteopaths, dance schools, ergonomic stores, pharmacists, maternal health centers or stores, corporations, etc.

You can find out who the person in charge is via phone, and either continue a conversation with that person or try to get a contact email, company address or email or make an appointment to talk to the owner or person in charge. The purpose of this is finding where your ideal client is and getting a professional referral.

Ask yourself what profession they are in, why would they refer clients to you? How would they find a massage therapist (what marketing source: social media, newspaper, internet, word of mouth, yellow pages etc...) and what would they want from a massage therapist for themselves or for their customers?

Start with smaller venues to get your feet wet and to build your confidence about talking to people. What I do is talk about the benefits of massage as a whole and let them ask about me specifically, which they will eventually do. Do not just sit at your booth and hope people will come. Just like everything else you must have an action plan. When things are quiet go to the other booths and introduce yourself, ask for a card and start a conversation.

Post event, you could offer a special of a complimentary 30min massage if they book within 2 weeks after the event. You can offer them an up-sell; get an hour massage for the additional charge of _____amount. You could offer free gifts---a bottle of peppermint oil, a free CD, etc. Use your imagination. And think about what you would like to have received and keep in mind your target market.

Decorate your booth with educational charts, like muscles, bones, trigger points, your sign of course, brochures of your business, stereo for music, table to display information and your table, sheets, towels, oil or lotion, if necessary.

You can do corporate massage to promote your business or some therapists focus only on corporations and massaging the employees. Look for health conscious businesses, suppliers of health related items, suppliers of fitness equipment. Usually younger companies are more responsive, companies with daycares, gyms, nutrition (lunch programs) for their employees. Again, keeping in mind who your TM is. If it is working with the elderly this may not be the right place to focus your attention.

Approach the HR manager, send him/her a letter with a brochure and business cards, and let them know how you can decrease their sick days by using your services. Go onto the internet and get your stats on the benefits of massage while working to reduce the number of sick days, increased productivity, stress reduction etc…

Always get contact information, phone number and email address. Follow up with them 2-3 days after their treatments and ask them how they felt during the treatment and after the massage. If they say they felt better after but no different on day 3, it gives you an opportunity to explain that this is normal and that with each consecutive treatment the pain should decrease either in intensity, frequency or duration. That is why you recommended the 4 consecutive treatments with one week in between each treatment, or whatever your treatment plan is.

After a few years in my clinic in Toronto I did a customer appreciation week in May since I realized that was my slowest month. I mailed out a letter to all my clients (back then computers and email wasn't the main source of communication) inviting them to book an appointment for a massage giving them a discount. I had a few clients come that week and some couldn't come that week, but the following week so it was well worth my efforts, it would be a great deal easier now with emails. I remember one client only came during that week and he usually booked a few treatments within in the month, as well; for him it was more about the price, although he enjoyed the treatments. My husband and I would laugh about it because every year we did the special, he would come just during that week or two during the year.

Make sure that instead of pushing the discount, push the benefit of massage (for them specifically) and what your massage will do, and make sure they get the best possible massage. That is why having a target market is so important because you can customize your message to that specific population and you get a better return on investment in your marketing.

Make sure that any print material you have, you leave them up where your ideal customer is for at least one to three months. Most people need to see something 7 times before they take action. Make sure there are no mistakes on your materials, spell check, check fonts, colour, header, telephone number, make sure everything is even and straight and uniform, email address, website and any social media links are included on your material.

STAY FOCUSED!

Ask yourself throughout the day, is what I am doing now leading me to... that next ideal customer, building my dream business, and taking me one step closer?

Simplify your goals so you can succeed in a lot of little steps instead of attempting to make huge leaps. A long series of little steps will get you where you want to go. DEFINE goals- 1. Determine TM 2. What marketing materials are you going to use? Flyers, postcards, face to face, corporation massage, sporting events, and etc. 3. Create the message targeting your ideal customer 4. Delivery of marketing

Concentrate all your efforts on those areas where you excel and outsource areas where you are weak. Remember that your time is money and if it takes 10 hours to do the same thing it might take someone else do in 2 hours; wouldn't it be worth paying someone for 2 hours? Remember to work out your Client's Lifetime Value; this will help here. Your hourly rate is probably more than the outsourcer and it will save you not only money, but you can focus your time on things that you like to do and other money generating activities.

If you need to hire others, then surround yourself with the best people you can find and then, get out of their way and let them do their job. Hire someone with a skill that you personally lack. When your business stalls or plateaus then you are usually keeping it stuck. When this happens, ask for help and it will move you beyond your own limitations (mentor, coach, mastermind group, friends). This will allow you to focus on the highest dollar-producing activity.

Focus on what your customer wants; not on what you want to see or feel that you would want to sell. Focus on finding the highest-quality customer. Know it is better to have 4 ideal customers than 40 mediocre ones because those 4 will generate referrals and help build your business and give you income throughout the year, not just one time.

Know that sales and marketing are key. Know that you are going to make mistakes; mistakes are a part of the learning curve. The key is to learn from your mistakes and if you can from other people's mistakes first. Put the mistakes behind you and move forward onto the next thing to do on your list.

Know that investing your time and energy at the beginning will pay dividends in the end, both personally and financially.

The best time to take action is **_right now._** Do not procrastinate by saying "I am going to take action once I put together the financing… or get around to it or find the right person." Do what you can right now and then put money aside for the next step in your plan, if it requires money. Taking action right now, according to Brian Tracey (Eat the Frog), is the best time because that's when you most want to do it.

Don't wait for the proverbial "better time" or "someday" there will never be the perfect time. I heard someone say the other day "someday"; is not on our calendars, it is not a name of a day of the week or a month or a year, so make today or Thursday, June 20, 2013, your day to start taking action towards turning your dream business into reality!

So now that you have figured out who your target market is, you have figured out how you are going to reach your TM (flyer, postcard, newspaper) and you have determined your CLV and, therefore, your marketing budget. Now it is time to go out and take action, stay focused on your vision of your dream business, keep working on overcoming your fears and keep doing the work you need to do to help grow your business. *Take ACTION everyday; it will pay off in the end!*

Much success! And if you feel like you got something from this book, then please recommend it to your colleagues, friends, family or business owners you know who may benefit from my experiences, my mistakes and my triumphs. Don't wait any longer, start NOW!

Please visit my Facebook page and leave a comment, pick up some tips and tricks and perhaps you can share with the community some your own. https://www.facebook.com/massageandmarketing

Resources

Recommended Books

Assaraf, John and Smith, Murray. *The Answer: Grow Any Business, Achieve Financial Freedom, and Live an Extraordinary Life.* New York, 2008

Proctor, Bob and Blood, Michelle. *Turbo Charged Goal Setting and Daily Action.* USA

Hill, Napoleon. *Think and Grow Rich.* USA, 1937

Roberts, Amy. *Ignite Your Massage Therapy Business Marketing Secrets for Massage Therapists.* Australia.

Wattles, Wallace. *The Science of Getting Rich, The Science of Being Well, and the Science of Being Great.* Pylon Publishing LLC, 1910

Byrne, Rhonda. *The Secret.* New York: Atria Books/Beyond Words, 2006

More Recommended Books

Canfield, Jack. *The Success Principles: How to Get from Where You Are to Where You Want to Be.* With Janet Spitzer. New York: Harper-Collins, 2005

Tracy, Brian. *Eat That Frog! 21 Great Ways to Stop Procrastinating and Get More Done in Less Time.* Jan 1, 2007

Sernovitz, Andy, Godin, Seth and Kawasaki, Guy. *Word of Mouth Marketing: How Smart Companies Get People Talking.* USA, Apr 26, 2012.

About the Author

Tina A. Hull, a wife and a Mother of two beautiful daughters; has worked within the health field for over 20 years. Tina has worked for large and small businesses. She has created, from scratch two successful massage therapy businesses in two very different locations. One was in the city of Toronto, where she was born and raised and the other on the island of Nevis, in the Caribbean.

Her goal with this book is to impart some lessons learned, sometimes the hard way of how to start, build and grow a small business.

"If I knew then, what I know now, my Massage Therapy Clinic in Toronto would have been even more successful!" states Tina.

If you are just graduating or beginning to start your own small business then this marketing book will help guide you. Don't wait until you are struggling to find ways to grow your business. Start with a solid, knowledge base, a strong foundation that will only improve your chances of success.

While, working in her own clinic, in Nevis, Tina started to take marketing more seriously. She began her journey and eventually earned her Certification as a Social Media Campaign Specialist and now is working on becoming a certified Publisher.

Tina's passion is to help people, whether that via massaging a client or via marketing to small business. She strives to help them to be the best they can be, and ultimately, to "turn their dream business into a reality!"

Contact Tina beyondexpectations688@gmail.com or Skype tina-hull. Much success in YOUR business!

A information can be obtained at www.ICGtesting.com

d in the USA

W10s2042190614

831LV00030B/1155/P

information can be obtained at www.ICGtesting.com
in the USA
10s2042190614

31LV00030B/1155/P